Social Change in
FRANCE

Social Change in
FRANCE

Michalina Vaughan
Martin Kolinsky
Peta Sheriff

ST. MARTIN'S PRESS · NEW YORK

Printed in Great Britain

First published in the United States of America in 1980

ISBN 0-312-73161-2

Library of Congress Cataloging in Publication Data

Clifford-Vaughan, Michalina.
  Social change in France.

  Bibliography: p.
  Includes index.
  1. France – Social conditions – 1945–   – Addresses,
essays, lectures.   2. Social change – Addresses, essays,
lectures.   I. Kolinsky, Martin, joint author.
II. Sheriff, Peta, joint author.   III. Title.
HN430.C5   1980   944   79-26695
ISBN 0-312-73161-2

Contents

Contents

Acknowledgements

The authors wish to thank the following institutions
which granted financial assistance: the Leverhulme
Trust, the Nuffield Foundation, the Canada Council.
Further assistance was provided by the Laboratoire
d'Economie et de Sociologie du Travail Aix-en-
Provence), by the Arts Research Committee of
McMaster University and under the Cultural
Exchange Program between Canada and France.
Organizational help and generous encouragement
were afforded by MM. Georges Graf, Louis Wetzel,
Marc Jeandet and Maurice Guyot, as well as
members of their respective staffs. Comments and
suggestions from Professor Alec Ross, Dr Gordon
Warwick, Dr Eva Kolinsky, Dr Coleman Romalis
and Dr Wallace Clement were greatly appreciated.
Our thanks are due to Marjorie Davies and Brenda
Wright who typed the manuscript. We would also like
to pay tribute to the patience of our families, friends
and neighbours who have suffered throughout the
lengthy preparation of this book.

Les régions et les départements

Source: La Documentation Française, *La Réforme Régionale*,
Notes et Etudes Documentaires No. 4064.

CHAPTER 1

Introduction

'The First Republic gave the French land, the Second gave them the vote, the Third gave them education' – at least this is how history used to be taught in state schools, even under the Vichy regime. Though clearly ideological and necessarily an over-simplification, such a view has the merit of highlighting some of the main features of French society from the Revolution onwards. First, the crucial importance of property relationships, derived from the abolition of feudal rights and formalized by the Code Napoléon, became a factor of socio-political stability, though it had revolutionary origins. It contributed to the recognition of agriculture as 'more than a special interest or merely one sector of the economy', as 'the very cornerstone of polity and society' (see p. 140). Second, equality tended to be defined in formal political rather than in socio-economic terms and radicalism was fully compatible, within the republican tradition, with the acceptance of authoritarian relationships, particularly in the work situation. Third, a meritocratic justification for social inequalities was provided by the Napoleonic system of secondary higher education, while the reforms of primary schooling under the Third Republic increased the chances of an able minority of gaining social promotion, mainly through entering the teaching profession. The 'connection between economic retardation, social persistence and educational continuity' (see p. 20), characteristic of pre-war France, could thus be related to the main political achievements of the three Republics and – perhaps more significantly, if less obviously – to their lack of

1

innovatory policies. The widespread belief that change could only be effected through revolutionary action – that it was the outcome of a crisis rather than of a planned process – appeared to be justified by the conservatism underlying radical rhetoric.

A number of explanations have been offered for this political conservatism. It is undoubtedly connected with the loss of energy exhibited by an ageing population. It is also partly derived from, and buttressed by, the institutional framework with which Napoleon endowed France. While they initially secured the achievements of the Revolution, the administrative and educational structures erected under the Empire constrained societal development to the extent that they concentrated the monopoly of initiative within the orbit of state intervention. They acted as a brake on economic development: 'French capitalism, protected behind customs barriers and exchange controls, successfully missed significant turning points in terms of technical advances' (see p. 88). Thus economic Malthusianism (the disregard of opportunities for growth) accentuated the effects of demographic stagnation.

Given this historical background, it is hardly surprising that a prolonged period of low vitality, aggravated by the losses of the First World War, should have led to the collapse of 1940. Nor is it astonishing that after the Liberation, when France embarked upon policies of modernization, they should have been delineated and implemented either by the state or under its auspices. The pressures, in response to which reforms were initiated, were experienced throughout Western Europe, since in all countries demographic expansion, sectoral reallocation and occupational repatterning occurred, albeit to varying extents.

France has its own special problems, but . . . its problems have a universal flavour. In fundamental respects, the issues faced by France today are typical of issues faced by most countries that are trying to respond simultaneously and in a coherent fashion to the pressures of population, the values of a traditional humanism, the requirements of democratic equality, and the needs of a sophisticated industrial economy. (OECD, 1972, pp. 17–18).

Cross-cultural comparisons prove illuminating in discussing educational expansion, for instance, 'new management' and administrative reforms aimed at deconcentration and participation. Though such parallels have occasionally been drawn in this book, the focus adopted is predominantly historical. Indeed, it is believed that the constant interplay between continuity and change characteristic of an old society cannot be understood without an exploration of characteristics inherited from the past. The persistence of such features either limits the scope or charts the course of modernizing policies. Even when issues have an 'international flavour', reforms are tackled within a socio-economic context and an institutional framework which are unmistakably French, the product of historical processes. Thus the administrative institutions within and through which change has taken place still bear a strong Napoleonic imprint, as the educational system did until 1968 and largely does even now. The extent of state powers, the expectation that they will be used to protect acquired rights and reliance on them to promote innovation are rooted in the past. The pervasiveness of central intervention, often denounced as crippling individual, group and local initiative, was recently diagnosed as an illness of French society, originating in the Napoleonic state. 'Since the state has taken over all powers, the French blame it for everything. Ordinary citizens, local representatives or civil servants, they consider the central power, to which they are subjected, as guilty of everything' (Peyrefitte, 1976, p. 302).

The inter-related features of administrative centralism, elitism in the civil service, bureaucratic remoteness from the public and hierarchical thinking, encouraged by the educational system which produces elites and influences managerial approaches, can all be traced back to the Napoleonic model. Demands for, attempts at and constraints on reform – whether designed to democratize recruitment to the higher civil service, to revitalize the regions, to expand education or to implement the somewhat elusive goal of participation – must be related to the historical background from which they emerged. Both the administrative structure and the educational system, having endured throughout the nineteenth century under successive political regimes, symbolized and ensured the continuity of the state and the stability of society under the Third Republic until the Second World War. After the collapse of the Vichy regime, they provided an institutional framework within which unprecedented pressures for quantitative expansion and qualitative adaptation had to be met. The former resulted from an extension of the tasks performed by the state through nationalization, economic planning and welfare service and, in the case of education, from increases in pupil/student intakes. The latter derived from a growing desire for a change in style, reconciling less authoritarian procedures with efficiency.

It is therefore essential to assess the contribution of the administrative and educational policies introduced under the Fourth and Fifth Republics to the modernization of contemporary France. The aptitude of administrators and of educators (who became civil servants under Napoleon and have always retained this status) to respond to a changed socioeconomic environment deserves special attention, because of their crucial responsibilities for social control. Designed by an authoritarian regime for a stable society, Napoleonic institutions were not suited to the pursuit of innovatory policies. Yet a hierarchical structure can provide an instrument for the planning and implementation of change by an elite committed to reformist goals. Such a commitment is a prerequisite, however, and cannot be imposed by governmental fiat on agents whose corporate interests and ideological tenets are challenged by the policies introduced. While higher civil servants furthered modernization, it had to be imposed upon reluctant academics, ambivalent about the implications for culture of growth and vocationalism and often opposed to reformist methods on ideological grounds. Differences in the values and attitudes of the elite group responsible for promoting planned social change are thus essential to the outcome of policies introduced 'from above'. Chapter 2 stresses that despite a series of reforms, and despite a crisis of quasi-revolutionary proportions, elite selection remains the main function of the educational system. The expansion imposed by demographic pressures has not adequately met rising social aspirations. Thus education mirrors a changed society more than it contributes to social change (Chapter 3). Yet the constraints of a strong heritage and of an elitist training for administrators notwithstanding, democratization of the higher civil service and administrative deconcentration have been pursued with some tenuous success, even if the more recent and less specific goal of citizens' participation remains largely theoretical (Chapter 4).

The pervasiveness of state intervention meant that the main sectors of the economy became enmeshed in a process of modernization at its instigation – despite the initial opposition of individual producers, particularly the smaller and less efficient ones, the persistent reluctance of some representative organizations and the profound distrust of the labour unions. The gradual acceptance of, and adaptation to, economic and technological pressures exerted by the *patronat* in an expanding industrial sector is analysed in Chapter 5. It is stressed, however, that the transformation of the traditional firm has not been accompanied by the institutionalization of dialogue between the two sides of industry. Chapter 6 interprets this failure in industrial relations by relating it to the tradition of revolutionary syndicalism in French working-class culture and the politics of a labour movement divided between competing unions.

Meanwhile the population engaged in the agricultural sector has diminished steadily. The contrast between the strength and adaptability to Common Market requirements of large-scale farming on the one hand and the extreme vulnerability of subsistence farming on the other has been summarized as the discrepancy between 'two agricultures'. Chapter 7 describes the political context in which this polarization has occurred, assesses its implications for the restructuring of rural society and focuses on its impact on regional development. The theme of the imbalance between areas of the country drained of manpower by rural exodus and fast-growing centres of economic activity and urban concentration is explored further in Chapter 8, together with demands and schemes for a more equitable distribution of resources.

While each chapter is signed by its author, whose views and

special interests it reflects, common themes run through all the
contributions, highlighting the constraints upon, and the scope
of, change within the areas investigated. Diagnosed in Chapter 4
and recurring throughout is the omnipresence of the state, with
the concomitant control of higher civil servants over the regulation of relationships between and to a large extent within
economic sectors, as well as in the educational system. Both in
the unprecedented expansion of the 1950s and in the current
climate of uneasy stabilization, the part played by the state can
be considered exceptionally important for a Western country.
The central planning – indicative rather than imperative – of
modernization has been the task of an administrative elite whose
members have also, with varying degrees of success,
endeavoured to spread their own views among other elite
groups. For the study of industrial development in a formerly
under-industrialized country, it is necessary to emphasize the
influence of state officials on managerial ideology (Chapter 5).
The painful adaptation of agriculture to the requirements of
capitalist production was facilitated by the close relationship
between officials and the leadership of young farmers (CNJA)
during the early 1960s, when new agricultural legislation was
framed (see Chapter 7). By contrast, no such co-operation was
sought with the trade unions, either in education or in industry.
Failure to involve the unions in the pursuit of the modernizing
goals and/or the reformist strategies of the state was diagnosed
by Jean Monnet, the author of French indicative planning, as the
flaw that could mar the whole attempt to transform the
economy. Writing to de Gaulle immediately after the Liberation,
he asserted:

> I am certain of one thing, that the French economy cannot be
> changed unless the French people participate in this trans-
> formation. By the people, I do not mean an abstract entity; I
> mean the trade unions, the industrialists, the administration,
> all the men who are associated with the implementation of a
> plan of equipment and modernization. (*Le Monde*, 6 April
> 1979)

Though no such consensus was secured, the Fourth Republic

could be said to have achieved not only post-war reconstruction, but also an economic 'take-off' conducive to a transformation of the employment market and a marked increase in living standards. 'The transition from semi-stagnation to growth . . . caused deep but generally acceptable change' (Dupeux, 1976, p. 218). The majority of the people accepted a mass-consumption society, despite the fact that the benefits derived from it varied considerably according to the socio-economic category and the region considered. Yet deep-rooted ideological divisions endured, so that the political right accepted modernization as a means towards greater affluence, while resenting and often opposing the new values associated with it, whereas the left tended to focus on redistribution rather than development (Zeldin, 1973). Resistance to the rationalizing pressures of growth by threatened small employers in industry and trade provided fuel for the 'Poujadist' movement in the early 1950s, undermining further an already weak, multi-party parliamentarian regime by depriving it of the support which the petite bourgeoisie had traditionally provided for the Third Republic (Hoffman, 1956).

Since it could neither ensure governmental stability nor solve the Algerian issue, the Fourth Republic fell victim to the parliamentary tradition and the colonialist legacy it had inherited. Though it failed to exorcise the past, it shaped the future by promoting the modernization on which the twin goals of the Fifth Republic depended. After de Gaulle's return to power, both the restoration of France's greatness in the international sphere and the promotion of national unity beyond ideological divisions implied that economic growth had now become a patriotic duty. Yet the consensus in which de Gaulle saw the source of his own legitimacy could only emerge in response to a sense of emergency. Its continuation in the medium term was threatened by the routinization of his charisma (Vaughan, 1976). The stability associated with a presidential regime and the attendant eclipse of party politics did not entail a reconciliation between conservatism and modernization. Nor did the benefits of affluence offset the tensions rooted in profound inequalities of distribution. Despite the wide appeal of nationalism, the presence of a widespread opposition was shown by the uneven appeal of Gaullism to various social categories, defined by reference to age, sex or occupation.

The electoral behaviour of younger voters, of industrial workers and of intellectuals, particularly women possessing high educational qualifications, appeared to foreshadow, in the early sixties, the basis on which the outburst of protest in 1968 was to be founded. As problems of adaptation to expansion were particularly acute in the educational system and within industry (in the small- and medium-sized firms – see pp. 93–4), the grievances of students and workers were accumulating. There were enough sources of discontent, with the rigidity of the state apparatus, the remoteness of decision-makers and the persistence of social inequalities, to account for the rapid spread of protest in May 1968. The deep-rooted belief that change could only be effected through crisis was a basic ingredient of the May movement: it perpetuated a revolutionary tradition enshrined in the teaching of French history. Thus its cultural origins are clear, as are some of the structural tensions which accounted for this 'incredible revolution' (Aron, 1968). In a sense, it is difficult to conceptualize the speed with which social control was regained unless considerable attention is paid to the objective contradictions that existed between the interests of the groups involved in protest. The contrast between the significant gains secured for workers through the Grenelle Agreement (see p. 129) and the 'vagueness . . . inseparable from political compromise' characterizing the Faure reform of higher education (see p. 26) highlights the divergence between the pursuit of greater shares in economic rewards on the one hand and the formulation of a participatory ideal on the other. Not only were the attacks of 1968 on 'consumerism' largely rhetorical, but they also disregarded the fact that workers' demands focused largely on securing higher living standards. Hence it is understandable that four years of accelerated growth should have followed, to which only the world energy crisis called a halt. It was the early seventies, after the first report of the Club of Rome and the

October War, that offered the first real challenge to expansionist policies (Drouin, 1979, p. 184): hence the contrast Drouin posits between this 'crisis' and the 'effervescence' of 1968.

If this dichotomy is accepted, structural changes may be expected to have ensued from the pressures of tougher competition among industrial economies, with its implications for the winnowing of inefficient firms and the spread of unemployment. Mere 'effervescence' yielded no such effects. After 1968 economic prosperity acted as a brake on labour unrest, while the official emphasis on participation served largely to contain conflict. Without indulging in any incursion into conspiracy theory, it is possible to construe the acceptance of participatory mechanisms as evidence of a 'spirit of prevention' on the part of administrators (see p. 84). After all, 'a political decision is not a solution; it is an arrangement' (de Jouvenel, 1963, p. 288). The history of French higher education since 1968 illustrates this point as sharply as that of the relationships between administrators and citizens. Thus an additional theme in this book is the resentment of authority structures and the concessions granted to reconcile diffuse desires for a greater share in decision-making with the persistence of existing hierarchies. The ambivalence of such egalitarian attitudes, coupled with a desire to secure state protection for the acquired rights of individuals and groups, as well as with a willingness to use administrative channels for upward mobility, is a characteristic derived from the pervasiveness of bureaucratic intervention in French history. Yet it ought not to be described as a cultural feature or related to imputations about 'national character' – a concept always invoked, according to Max Weber, as a substitute for structural explanation (Gerth and Mills, 1970, p. 64). Such ambivalent attitudes clearly derive from the institutional arrangements discussed mainly in Chapters 2 to 4 and from the effects of economic retardation analysed in Chapters 5 to 8.

This emphasis on inequalities of power and responses to them is not reducible to class analysis, though it endeavours to incorporate some of the insights yielded by such an approach. Indeed, a classical economic crisis might well be conducive to the phenomena of polarization which stimulate class consciousness and result in class conflict. However, despite the unrest of 1968, social change under the Fourth and Fifth Republics has been planned rather than crisis-induced; it has been evolutionary and not revolutionary. Its main source can be identified as the policies of the state, implemented by an administrative elite linked (especially through education) with other elite groups, on which it has tended to impose its style of modernizing activity. Consequently, power differentials have been perceived as a crucial form of inequality, although demands for the wider diffusion of influence have not escalated into attacks on the existence of hierarchies – perhaps as a result of the general acknowledgement of meritocratic legitimation. In this respect the role of the educational system as a mechanism of social control, justifying inequalities of power and rewards within an industrial society, cannot be overstressed.

However, to focus on these features of social reality entails a neglect of other sources and forms of both persistence and change. The family has not been discussed either as a socializing institution or as an agency for the transmission of property, except in so far as social origins relate to educational attainments (Chapter 3). A concentration on planned social change rather than on social movements has precluded the analysis of militancy, whether within political parties, the women's liberation movement, the progressive section of the Catholic Church or the *autonomiste* fringe. Unions and professional associations are referred to as supporters of (or, more often, as antagonistic to) bureaucratically designed reforms, but their structure and bureaucratization have not been investigated. These are the drawbacks inherent in highlighting the centrality of state action* and the significance of the bureaucratic model, as well as the influence of the administrative elite. The extent to which these factors emphasize persistence within change and link conservatism to innovation appears to justify the perspective

---

*For an alternative, more voluntaristic interpretation of the evolution experienced by French society, see Wright, 1978.

adopted in this study. Thus to focus on the management or the initiation of change by the state is to acknowledge that enduring inequalities of power remain characteristic of French society.

BIBLIOGRAPHY

ARON, R. (1968) *La révolution introuvable. Réflexions sur le mouvement de mai* (Paris: Fayard).
DROUIN, R. (1979) *Qu'est-ce qui fait courir la France?* (Paris: Plon).
DUPEUX, G. (1976) *French Society 1789–1970* (London: Methuen).
GERTH, H. and MILLS, C. W. (1970) *From Max Weber* (London: Routledge & Kegan Paul).
HOFFMAN, S. (1956) *Le mouvement Poujade* (Paris: Colin).
JOUVENEL, B. de (1963) *De la politique pure* (Paris: Calmann-Lévy).
O.E.C.D. (1972) *Educational Policy and Planning* (Paris).
PEYREFITTE, A. (1976) *Le mal français* (Paris: Plon).
VAUGHAN, M. (1976) 'Gaullism', in M. Kolinsky and W. E. Paterson (eds.), *Social and Political Movements in Western Europe* (London: Croom Helm).
WRIGHT, V. (1978) *The Government and Politics of France* (London: Hutchinson).
ZELDIN, T. (1973) *Conflicts in French Society* (London: Allen & Unwin).

CHAPTER 2

Elite Selection and Educational Reforms

Michalina Vaughan

FOUNDATIONS, TRENDS, STRESSES AND STRAINS

Discussions of educational change in contemporary France generally tend to be related to the events of 1968. Yet this date is not the true beginning of student protests, merely an escalation of tensions experienced throughout the years of overcrowded educational establishments and unmanageable educational reforms under the Fourth and early Fifth Republics. Nor is it the starting point of staff protest. Indeed, professional associations of academics and teachers had resisted reforms on behalf of the threatened cultural standards, and with some thought for their members' threatened vested interests, ever since the Third Republic (for example, under the ministry of Jean Zay). Nor can the *loi d'orientation*, originating from the compromise reached in Parliament in 1968, be considered a true educational solution. Its implementation is still susceptible to considerable changes and its very nature makes it fluid. For this reason 1968 was neither the beginning of the end of educational struggle nor the end of the beginning of educational reorganization. It could best be described as a crucial experience in the consciousness of several generations – assuming that students and teachers belong to more than one generation, as was generally the case in the professoriate-dominated faculties of the time. This made it a landmark in individual biographies rather than a culminating point in the evolution of the French educational system. During the purely educational phase of the 'troubles' – that is, while protest escalated from Nanterre to the Sorbonne – a series of happenings might well have been mistaken for genuine events. This should not prevent one from stressing, with hindsight, the importance of the two subsequent stages. During the economic stage, strike action involved some eight million technical, professional and industrial workers for approximately twelve days (15–27 May). During the political stage, in late May and early June, political parties and trade unions displayed considerable skill in tension management and the regaining of control. The initial phase was the triggering off of a crisis which almost appeared capable of attaining revolutionary proportions. Yet the degree of worker support for the student cause was insufficient to ensure a cohesive blend between political protest and academic idealism. The popular *fête* was a vital part of the French revolutionary tradition, but the revolutionaries of 1789 had begun by storming the Bastille. In 1968 the *fête* was, in a sense, a substitute for action among intellectuals – whereas professionals, workers and bureaucrats, whether in the state machinery or in the unions, had more precise claims and more definite expectations.

It is thus logical to consider the educational crisis revealed by the first stage of the 1968 events as pertaining to a series of tensions experienced by the French educational system. They had gained momentum for about half a century, ever since plans for the reform of the Napoleonic framework had been given increasingly serious consideration in political and academic circles. To interpret student protest in the context of educational history does not amount to a rejection of other causes for discontent within their generation on grounds indirectly related or even unrelated to their work situation. It merely focuses the explanation of the first (purely educational) phase of the May events on those conditions which actually brought the students and some of the staff out of the campus and on to the streets. These conditions were inseparable from the organization of education throughout the nineteenth century and thus incomprehensible without some historical preamble.

The Napoleonic framework of elite selection

The university, one and indivisible like the Republic of which Napoleon had crowned himself emperor, subordinated research to teaching and defined education as serving the needs of the state rather than as an end in itself (Vaughan and Archer, 1971). From Paris the Ministry of Education ruled the local universities, which were no more than assemblages of faculties (without always including the full range of these). It appointed and promoted staff, allocated finance and, most important, set curricula, thereby ensuring a strict uniformity of teaching throughout the whole country. Qualifications were thus interchangeable, whatever particular faculty had granted them, as a corollary of the state monopoly of all degrees and grades. The faculties of law, medicine and theology were mere training establishments, through which the state exercised control over entry into the corresponding professions and the civil service. By contrast, the faculties of arts and of sciences had minimal teaching and research functions, but a major involvement in examining for the *baccalauréat* or secondary leaving cerfiticate. The close connection between higher and secondary education was thus an initial feature of the system, as were the symbolic and social significance of the *baccalauréat* and the relative lack of prestige of the faculties (as mere ante-rooms to future occupational life). After the defeat of 1870 and its attribution, by such writers as Taine and Renan, to the superiority of German scientific training and pedagogy, a measure of administrative and financial autonomy was granted to the universities, formally re-established under that name by the law of 1896. However, this half-hearted attempt at reform really consisted in granting universities the legal status of *établissements publics* and emancipated them slightly from the Ministry's tutelage (for example, in the event of a trial), but it did not undermine centralization or encourage either originality or regionalism (Zeldin, 1967, pp. 59–60). These enduring features of the Napoleonic university remained unaltered by the legislation of the Third Republic (Prost, 1968, p. 223) and have been perceived as major stumbling blocks to successive educational reforms since the end of the Second World War.

An equally lasting and no less controversial legacy of the Napoleonic system is the existence of *grandes écoles* (such as the *Ecole Polytechnique* for mathematics and engineering and the *Ecole Normale* for arts and sciences), designed to provide an elite of highly trained civil servants. These institutions, created during the Revolution but refounded by Napoleon, were intended to be both meritocratic and vocational. These two features, as well as their close connection with the administrative hierarchy, epitomized the philosophy of the regime. The level of knowledge expected and tested at entry, the quality of the tuition given and the final grading of pupils by competitive examination (the *concours de sortie*, which is the counterpart of the *concours d'entrée*) conferred on these institutions greater prestige than that enjoyed by any other educational establishment. Their former pupils retained – and still do – the title of *ancien élève* for life, since it has always been held more desirable than any university degree and has guaranteed access to positions entailing higher social and material rewards. The persistence of the *grandes écoles* alongside the faculties and their differential prestige rating has ensured the perpetuation of a meritocratic elite. It has also provided a model for devising new schools where new types of elites could be trained. The ENA (see Chapter 4) is a case in point. Thus 'the state continues, perhaps even to a greater extent than in the nineteenth century, to train its own public service elite . . . (which) spills over into the private sector' (Suleiman, 1978, p. 25).

The obvious penalty of this elitism is that unless efforts are made to equalize initial opportunities, the rewards of manifest ability tend to be restricted to the members of certain social groups. Meanwhile the existence of latent aptitudes in others is almost bound to remain undiscovered. It seems fairly obvious that from their inception the bias of the faculties towards a bourgeois intake was inseparable from the need for parents to cover living expenses and fees during the undergraduate course. The *grandes écoles*, whose pupils acquired the status of civil servants at entry and were therefore remunerated, represented an important avenue of social mobility for gifted individuals throughout the nineteenth and early twentieth centuries.* However, access to preliminary instruction and coaching for the entry *concours* were necessary prerequisites. Hence the special advantage enjoyed by the sons of primary school teachers, whose home environment offered the appropriate incentives and facilities. The emergence of this meritocratic intellectual elite – compensating in some respects for the exclusiveness of the French educational system – is the asset resulting from a constant emphasis on selection by merit. The correlative liabilities will become more obvious in the following chapter.

Outside the meritocracy

From the start, the channelling of limited resources in personnel and finance into establishments of secondary and higher standard was among the liabilities of the system. Napoleon's neglect of primary schooling, abandoned to the Catholic Church – provided elementary morality and dynastic loyalty were inculcated in the masses – was compatible with his own elitism. Yet it contradicted the secularism inherent in eighteenth-century philosophy which the new elites of post-revolutionary France had absorbed. Despite temporary gains under the Restoration and the Second Empire (such as the famous *loi Falloux*), the clergy's struggle against the degree-granting monopoly of the university was ultimately a rearguard action. Republican policy, linking secularism and social control, culminated in the creation of a free and compulsory system of primary instruction in the

---

*Ringer (1979, pp. 180–190) analyses studies of the social origins of *grandes écoles* graduates to show that this channel for upward mobility was available, especially for the lower middle class, throughout the nineteenth century. However, *Ecole Polytechnique* remained socially exclusive until the 1880s.

1880s. The *écoles normales*, where primary teachers were trained, provided an avenue of upward mobility for the most gifted children of the peasantry, as well as a breeding ground for secularism. The influence on the rural population of the *hussars noirs de la République*, as these teachers were nicknamed, and their frequent competition with parish priests for prestige and power at the village level, became instruments of educational change and of political polarization under the Third Republic (Archer, 1979, p. 318). The contribution of primary schooling to a gradual process of social promotion, mainly conducive to rural exodus, cannot be isolated from the politically divisive effects of the religious controversy over education, widening the gulf between left and right. It would be naive – as André Siegfried and a number of his followers have shown – to define religiously motivated anti-republicanism as the prerogative of privileged social strata such as the landed gentry, or to equate the 'catchment area' of Catholic education with the offspring of families belonging to this milieu. Historical rather than social criteria might well be essential to account for the dechristianization of southern France and for the entrenchment of the Church in the west and the east. With regard to educational choice as well as to voting behaviour, regional differences cut across social barriers.

Elite culture

The late development of secular primary schooling under the Third Republic perpetuated the Napoleonic tradition of an inferior status for the establishments conveying minimal knowledge to the masses. The social origins and intellectual background of primary teachers accentuated the division between educational levels, since elementary instruction was isolated from the interpenetrating worlds of secondary and higher education, which largely remained the preserve of the bourgeoisie. The much respected *agrégation*, granted by faculties of sciences and of arts, which was the certificate required of *lycée* teachers, symbolized the divide. Contrary to what optimistic egalitarians might have expected, the steady increase in the number of *agrégés* during the first half of the twentieth century widened the gulf which separated primary schools from the remainder of the educational system, to the extent that the intellectual level of secondary instruction rose. Thus major figures representative of French philosophical and political thought – such as Bergson, Alain and Sartre – taught in *lycées* rather than in universities and ensured the continuity of a common academic culture on both sides of the *baccalauréat*. This was not only a 'barrier' (since only the *bacheliers* could gain entry into higher education), but also a 'level' (Goblot, 1925), the guarantee of having reached cultural standards considered to be essential for university entrants and for 'cultivated' members of the privileged classes. This kind of cultivation was not available to primary teachers, let alone their pupils. The description of certain individuals as *primaires* implied a shade of contempt for the possession of certain kinds of knowledge and the excessive care displayed in conveying it to others, in imparting mere information. The difference between this kind of tuition and that dispensed at secondary level would best be summarized by the stress on *agrégation*, which guaranteed that teachers would have 'an exemplary type of mind' rather than that they would merely teach a subject. In fact, the uniformizing pressures of the *agrégation* programmes were more influential in preserving the standardized, regionally undifferentiated and socially predictable character of French education than the subordination of all teaching establishments to one central ministry. They delineated and enforced the concept of culture characteristic of French academe. The *agrégés* were too deeply committed to this concept not to resent in advance any attempt at reform which would modernize or, in their view, dilute it. It goes without saying that they had also acquired rights to protect it and that, in terms of personal prestige, they resented any attempt at severing the connection established between the *lycées* and the faculties through the *baccalauréat* as a test of pupils' mental aptitude to receive higher education.

A major obstacle to the adaptation of the Napoleonic system

to twentieth-century pressures for greater egalitarianism and for updated vocationalism (that is, a more responsive attitude towards demands for increased numbers of people trained to perform more complex tasks) has consistently been found in the commitment of the teachers themselves to the Napoleonic concept of the university, integrating *lycées* and faculties in one network, with which the primary system is not connected. Breaking the mould into which culture itself was set was implicit in any restructuring of the relationships between the different types of instruction, the institutions in which they were imparted and the staff who were responsible for conveying them to the respective intake. Attachment to tradition and enlightened self-interest would be oversimplified explanations for the durability of the Napoleonic system, despite the manifestly obsolete character of the isolation inflicted on primary schools. The truth is that this system had been conceived as elitist to meet the quantitatively limited and qualitatively well-defined needs of a pre-industrial country for administrative, professional and teaching cadres. While it was obviously unable to cope with the exigencies of twentieth-century society, it retained a prestige which equated its content with the very quality of French culture. Consequently, egalitarian pressures for the closing of the gap between primary and secondary education (or, to put it more explicitly, for the elimination of primary forms from secondary establishments and for the setting up of a 'middle school', enabling selection to take place at a later age) clashed with legitimate concern for the preservation of cultural standards. Nor was this concern exclusive to the professional providers of education, whether at the secondary or at the higher level, or even to those social strata whose offspring were the main beneficiaries of the existing mechanisms of selection. To the extent that educational mobility was a plurigenerational process, the primary teachers had a vested interest in the preservation of an elitist system which ensured that their own children or, at the very worst, their grandchildren reached the apex of the *grandes écoles*.

Attention has often been drawn to the stability of the

administrative structures set up under the Empire to which French education belonged (at least above primary level) and for which it catered. The slow pace of industrialization, at least until the 1950s, was a contributory factor in delaying the outburst of an ultimately unavoidable crisis (see Chapter 5). This connection between economic retardation, social persistence and educational continuity has been strikingly described as *'stabilité socio-scolaire'* (Charles Morazé, 1966)). Yet one of the major reasons why the stability of schools outlasted that of society was that there was widespread adherence to a formal definition of culture which assumed it to be at least as constraining as, and probably more deeply internalized than, the structural context within which it had initially evolved. The retention of elitism, like the perpetuation of uniformity, was inseparable from the logic of centralization, but they were both to a large extent produced by a traditionalism that equated the French educational past with the former supremacy of the national culture.

Alternative modes of selection

This is not tantamount to denying that pressures for reform were made in the inter-war period, under the impetus of the *Compagnons de l'Université Nouvelle*. Indeed, they were outlined in some detail in the Bill tabled by Jean Zay as Minister of Education in 1937 and partially implemented (as *classes d'orientation*)* until the war of 1939. However, elitism helps account for the resistance to setting up an *école unique*, along comprehensive lines, as a bridge between primary and secondary cycles of instruction and to postponing selection into the middle-school stage. After the Vichy interlude, during which secularization regressed and Catholic schools were subsidized (but no constructive reform was even considered), the Fourth Republic resumed the practice of its predecessor. Its educational policy could best be described as a prolonged and complex

---

*These *classes*, actually introduced in fifty towns, corresponded to the first year of secondary school and were meant to guide pupils towards classical, modern or technical streams grouped within the same school.

exercise in evading decision-making. Demographic pressures due to the post-war bulge, entailing a massive growth in educational intakes, and the requirements of an expanding economy led to a multiplication of programmes. The well-known Langevin–Wallon plan, which split up schooling into three stages (until 11, followed by guidance until 15 and then vocational or academic training until 18) proved too radical in 1947. Proposals – supported by the various teachers' unions and associations and influenced by their respective professional interests – to channel pupils into short or long streams at the end of primary schooling, at the beginning of secondary schooling or in the course of an overlap phase, were much discussed in the National Assembly in the early fifties. They proved abortive in the absence of overall educational reform. The concept of two secondary cycles, one short and one long, was becoming increasingly acknowledged as a necessity. However, the unreserved support of the educators who would have to implement it somehow, either in distinct establishments or on both sides of the primary/secondary divide, was lacking. Conflict between vested interests, governmental instability and the unwillingness of political parties to attribute a high priority to an electorally divisive issue meant further procrastination. Neither André Marie's two-year orientation cycle to be held in all schools nor Billères' middle school* could silence the passionate pleas in favour of preserving selection procedures for the sake of elite recruitment. The reluctance to sacrifice cultural standards for the sake of adaptation to a modern economy effectively concealed the anti-egalitarianism inherent in advocating an unchanged, unabridged, 'undiluted' secondary education. Elitism was defended on grounds of quality – the equivalent English slogan at the time was 'More means worse'. In practice, it would certainly have meant 'different', and the built-in assumption was that change could only be for the worse, since the traditional university symbolized a type of perfection. Meanwhile the practical situation deteriorated. As the intake of

*Variations on Zay's concept of *classes d'orientation*, extended to two years in the first case and to three in the second (Fraser, 1963, p. 8).

higher education increased by 14 per cent a year between 1962 and 1967, overcrowding made university teaching virtually unmanageable, particularly in Paris. Contradictory views held by academics about the respective claims of excellence and vocationalism were expressed with increasing acrimony.

The advent of the Fifth Republic officially ushered in a policy of institutional reform and the discontinuation of concessions on grounds of political expediency. The new regime upheld modernization and economic growth, if need be at the expense of the scruples exhibited by intellectuals, whose political stance tended to be anti-Gaullist anyway. The choice of the Minister of Education, Fouchet, whose term of office (1963 to April 1967) outlasted that of any previous incumbent, was characteristically provocative. His former experience had been military and political and, as a man of action, he was uninhibited by traditionalism or excessive respect for academic culture. Nor was he daunted by the prospect of heading 'the biggest enterprise in the world apart from the Red Army' – to quote the colourful words with which he conveyed the fact that his ministry was actually the biggest employer of manpower in France. He was determined to enforce change, even at the risk of upsetting officialdom and of horrifying educationalists. With typically military humour, M. Fouchet commented: 'In fact the university does not mind so much being raped' (*Le Monde*, 9–10 April 1967). Perhaps rape did not appear sufficiently unavoidable to be enjoyed in 1968. Still, the early phase of reforms between 1963 and 1966 certainly offered a favourable contrast to the indecisiveness of the Fourth Republic over issues of selection.

The Fouchet policy was to offer alternative outlets to pupils unable or unwilling to follow the traditional academic course leading from the *lycée* to higher education by providing short courses relevant to future careers or jobs. This was a necessary outcome as compulsory school attendance was lengthened and as employers and parents alike exhibited a more positive attitude about the level of instruction required in a modern society. The tide of secondary entrants could not be expected to gain the *baccalauréat*, with its historical emphasis on the classical and unapplied subjects and the built-in right for its holders to register in any university. The 'myth' of the *baccalauréat* as prerequisite for social respectability and occupational success was to be gradually undermined by the process of turning terminal forms into specialized sections whose work led to different examinations and corresponding future academic studies. In the longer term it was hoped to break down the monopoly of the *baccalauréat* as a channel to all desirable forms of employment – though it was politically infeasible to deprive it of its status as a passport to university entrance. Only the *grandes écoles* – thanks to their reliance on a *concours d'entrée* – could retain their traditional selectivity. The faculties were bound to compensate somehow for the absence of a pre-entry selection; hence the creation of cycles. The first provided basic training in the arts or the sciences and culminated in a diploma. The second introduced specialization up to either *licence* or master level, while the third consisted of research work for a thesis. The purpose was to maintain standards without denying the possibility of opting for shorter alternatives, which could be viewed as terminal. Comparable solutions had been introduced in the law faculties in the late fifties, while both medical and pharmaceutical faculties devised preparatory years for entrants. Increasingly the burden of selection was being shifted onto the faculties, despite the problems of numerically inadequate staff and deficient material facilities. The gap between *grandes écoles* and universities was thus widened, and the disadvantages of graduates in relation to *anciens élèves* from the viewpoint of future careers were maximized. Reforms intended as democratic and vocational failed completely to compete with the time-honoured forms of elite selection by *concours*. This process of modernization, of necessity slow and rendered harsher by the lack of amenities in the new campus universities (especially those located around Paris, among which Nanterre was to become famous), was also hampered by the requirements of educational centralization. A completely fixed curriculum, imposed on new, often literally unfinished establishments, provided a constant source of irritation. The May movement is more understandable when placed in this setting, even though it is not reducible to such relatively minor causes.

Corresponding reforms at secondary level entailed a challenge to the dichotomy between *lycées* and the post-primary forms located in other establishments whose staff were non-graduate teachers. The formerly unbridgeable division between these types of schooling was to be overcome by gradual comprehensivization and by an emphasis on the 'middle years'. It was at that stage that the observation of pupils would lead to their being channelled into the stream corresponding to their potential and aspirations. The following chapter will concentrate on the multiplication of educational hurdles inherent in this system. It will stress the degree of fit between family background and school assessment, which culminates in a predictable connection between the social origins and the aptitudes posited, exhibited and/or detected. At this stage it suffices to point out that the coexistence of *lycées* and *collèges* (the CESs of the Berthoin reform in 1959 and the CETs of the Fouchet 1963–4 phase) was not facilitated by the competition between their personnel and the corresponding associations. Nor was it helped by the determination of families endowed with sufficient knowledge and influence to secure the more advantageous location for their children – that is, to avoid the shorter and more narrowly vocational courses. Discontent was rampant at secondary level; in May 1968 it became rife at university level. Pupil protest, though neither as massive nor as effective as its student counterpart, loomed large in a number of establishments, including some of the most renowned *lycées* of Paris. An additional confirmation was thus given to the theory that protest too was an elite prerogative. It may have been associated with youth – a fact hardly surprising, given demographic pressures in a country where in the mid-sixties there were twice as many people under 25 as in 1939, although the population as a whole had only risen by 27 per cent. It was, in fact, a prerogative of the privileged young, of those who had been selected rather than rejected.

Loi d'orientation: REFORM OR REGRESSION?

The events of 1968 called the attention of the world to the complex web of traditionalism and reform in which French education was entangled. They did not bring the Gaullist reliance on reformism to an end. Pompidou, who was beginning to emerge as more representative of the Gaullist stance than the General himself, claimed that 'things will never be the same again' (Archer, 1977, p. 75). Yet the appointment of a new Minister of Education, Edgar Faure, whose brief was to call a working party in order to prepare a reform of higher education, showed the government's determination to impose a compromise solution. Nor were the criticisms of the existing system made by the working party of startling originality. They focused on the rigidity of centralization, on the attendant resistance to innovation – whether structural or pedagogical – and on the excessive importance attributed to examinations. The seeds of all these failings could be found in the Napoleonic university. However, the decision actually to dismantle it was not contained in the *loi d'orientation de l'enseignement supérieur*, whose inspiration could be traced to a round table of academics from the science faculties held in Caen in 1966 on the theme of university modernization (Bourricaud, 1977, p. 12–6). There was no break with the main proposals put forward and contemplated under the Fouchet ministry. The greater willingness to experiment with their more controversial aspects was induced by the need to placate student opinion and its supporters among academics as well as those outside academe. The law was intended to effect a compromise between those who meant to draw far-reaching conclusions from the discontent evidenced in May and those who believed or hoped that a minimum amount of change would suffice now that order had been restored in France. It would be an oversimplification to assume that the supporters of these incompatible interpretations were split along the traditional divide between the left and the right. Change could be seen mainly as a greater emphasis on vocationalism, a view popular with administrators, firmly held by employers and supported by the less politicized students. Alternatively, it could be construed as an attempt to implement democratization by widening the social recruitment of the student body and by increasing its share – as well as that of junior and non-tenured staff – in decision-making processes. The latter attitude could not really be described as characteristic of the political left, since the *gauchistes* opposed the law in principle. Furthermore, many traditionalist university teachers who belonged to what could be described as the 'old' republican left rejected modernization on cultural grounds, without necessarily avowing their vested interest in doing so. On the right the cleavage was between the technocrats, committed to vocational relevance, and the die-hard conservative right, who equated reform with the unleashing of chaos. The near-unanimity of Parliament in adopting the law in November 1968 – with only the communists and six Gaullists, Fouchet included, abstaining – shows that the need for an urgent decision was widely felt in the aftermath of May. It confirms also that the provisions enacted appeared sufficiently elastic to allow for a variety of subsequent decisions. Vagueness is inseparable from political compromise involving numerous partners pursuing divergent ends. It is certainly characteristic of many, if not most, provisions of the *loi d'orientation*.

The main principle underlying the Faure reform – as it should properly be called, if only because of the Minister's strong influence on the content of the law he pushed through Parliament – is that of university autonomy. This can be considered, and has sometimes been described as, a relinquishment of the Napoleonic concept, the beginning of a new era in French higher education. 'The chairs and the *facultés* integrated in over twenty languid universities were abolished and replaced by more than 600 *Unités d'Enseignement et de Recherche* [UERs, the rough equivalent of American departments] which, between 1969 and 1971, regrouped themselves into sixty or so [now seventy-five] interdisciplinary and autonomous universities' (Fomerand, 1977, p. 94). The reform could be perceived as a political move, disconnecting those in power from the university authorities and thus ensuring that any future student protest would remain a campus matter rather than escalating into a national issue. This somewhat Machiavellian view (Aron, 1976, p. 414) is compatible with the notion that academics themselves could be relied on to assert their traditionalism in any institutional context and to recreate a closed corporative universe (Bourricaud, 1977, p. 4). A less pessimistic approach stresses that autonomy is limited by the government's financial control. The Ministry of Education provides the yearly budget of each university, which has no other source of funds, and it covers the cost of all major building and equipment projects. Within budgetary limits there is freedom to spend, as well as freedom to draw up statutes and to decide on administrative matters. Though established posts, whose holders have the status of civil servants, are filled by ministerial decision, the universities concerned have gained the right to be consulted. The powers of the Minister for Universities have recently been increased to include the transfer of posts from one university to another, after consultation with the establishments concerned, and the transfer of unestablished staff (*Le Monde*, 9 June 1978). While there is a quantitative limitation on student intake (influenced, no doubt, by the fear of protest on too large a scale and also by the general discontent latent in the vast campuses created in the sixties), the law does not actually refer to a ceiling. The parliamentary debate preceding its adoption referred to a maximum of 2500 students per UER, though not to any limit to the number of UERs per university. Financial and staffing constraints currently regulate intakes. Despite some limitations, a measure of flexibility in administrative and pedagogical matters now exists, by contrast with the earlier pattern of enforced uniformity (Archer, 1979, p. 665).

A directive for its implementation has been laid down in the second principle underlying the law, namely multi-disciplinarity. While it was recognized that some universities would be specialized, the desirability of a cross-fertilization between literary and scientific disciplines was strong was strongly urged. Although all university degrees must be national ones, authorized by the state through the Ministry of Education, some scope for innovation in the design of courses that straddled archaic barriers between the former faculties was offered. This could theoretically result in the emergence of original, multi-disciplinary UERs, provided the desire for innovation was strong and unhampered by political enmities or intellectual superciliousness. Duverger points out that the law faculties had undergone a major reorganization in 1954, under the influence of a pressure group composed of imaginative academics. They had modernized their curricula and had provided for the gradual emancipation of economics and politics from the former hegemony of Roman and civil law. He contrasts the results which could be achieved by determined individuals with the attachment to the *status quo* and the lack of enterprise generally exhibited in the context of the Faure reform. 'Some interesting innovations here and there [were] submerged in a general return to the past' (Duverger, 1977, p. 216). Indeed, the staff meetings which decided (with student participation or without, depending on the political climate prevailing locally) how the ex-faculties were to be dismantled and what new units would emerge in their place, showed remarkably little zeal for multi-disciplinarity. The dominant trend was towards centring on one discipline and remaining among familiar colleagues. This was achieved either by merely renaming the faculty a UER, as was common in the smaller university towns, or by making the units coincide with major courses taught or even with the chairs existing before 1968. The alternative solution, that of making the units coincide with cycles of study, proved much less popular. Reasons of prestige dissuaded academics from teaching juniors only, and there was genuine concern about the separation between teaching and research inherent in this plan. It is only in a minority of cases that multi-disciplinary teaching has been introduced. Somewhat paradoxically, it was Minister Edgar Faure who decided that three centres for modern studies should operate in the region of Paris: in the already notorious Nanterre, in Vincennes (whose fame for extremism was to spread rapidly) and in Paris VII. In the absence of an overall plan, particularly for the subdivision of the huge University of Paris, where 200,000 students were registered in 1968, and also for that of the main provincial universities, academics were left in a position somewhat reminiscent of feudalism. Each professor could take his chair to the university of his choice in the cities where several emerged and, in doing so, he enabled it to retain the post for ever ('Offices were becoming hereditary' – Duverger, 1977, p. 225), and there was acute competition to secure the allegiance of 'old mandarins', as well as to grab the best buildings. In this unedifying scramble complementarity between subject matters and/or between world views naturally prevailed over multi-disciplinarity. The split of the old Sorbonne between two different universities along strictly political lines was a case in point, as was the concentration of four-fifths of the former *Faculté de Droit* in the new Paris II, while the remainder of their colleagues joined other social scientists in Paris I. A measure of what the students had called 'integration' in their 1968 manifestos was achieved in some establishments, but the ideal of multi-disciplinarity was defeated. Arguably, it might have been imposed by direct governmental intervention, but this would, no doubt, have been a widely unpopular measure, eliciting charges of Fascism from the most diverse quarters, and might conceivably have been doomed to failure anyway, since Utopias are not easily established by unbelievers.

In any case, the most politically sensitive issue was not pedagogic, but organizational. Hence it was the third principle embodied in the *loi d'orientation*, the participation of students and junior staff in the governance of universities, that was covered by the most detailed provisions and whose implementation was most attentively watched by all interested parties. The initial expectation of parity between staff and students in the councils of the UERs was rapidly reduced to make way for the acquired rights of the professoriate, whithout denying other academics an opportunity to be heard. Allowing for the possibility of waivers granted by the Ministry of Education to take account of local conditions, the unestablished university teachers were given 40 to 50 per cent of the staff representation, while the professors and *maîtres de conférences* usually retained a majority within it. The ratio of two staff representatives to one student representative was justified by the assumption that the staff did not make up one constituency – and indeed their work situation and career prospects are widely different. Further restrictions were also introduced as to the areas in which student participation was allowed. Financial decisions, matters of appointment and promotion and, more controversially, the content of curricula, the testing of knowledge, as well as all selection devices were excluded. In addition, the student body was not considered to be a single constituency any more than the staff. First-year undergraduates could only elect one delegate in five in units offering a course of more than two years' duration, and only the representatives of students registered for third-cycle courses were entitled to a share in the management of research centres. Yet participation has been inhibited less by the legalism of the arrangements laid down by the Faure reform than by the reluctance of the students themselves to play an active role in the councils. Politicized students are unwilling to accept the Gaullist ideology of participation (see Chapter 4), while uncommitted ones are more inclined to apathy than to devotion of vast amounts of time to attendance at lengthy, verbose, frequently inconclusive council meetings. Thus the student population has on the whole failed to become involved in the games for which such a complicated system of rules has been devised.* The representativeness of student delegates has, in fact, been challenged by moderates and, of course, by the right, in a situation where the average percentage of voters in university elections is 25 per cent. The presence in the councils of outsiders invited to represent major national and regional interests has been challenged by the left as a concession to employers and, generally, to *les notables*. Yet it has also been denounced by the more modernistic academics as a missed opportunity for overcoming the isolation of the university from

---

*The inability of student unions to channel the aspirations of politicised students seeking to change capitalist society rather than to defend their interests within the academic system of this society is highlighted by Touraine (1978, p. 357). This explanation should be taken into account as a corrective to the frequent emphasis on student apathy.

the wider society. The issues discussed by the councils are generally too narrow – centring as they do on timetabling, the use of lecture rooms, the deployment of staff or the spending of financial allocations – to stimulate the interest of laymen or to allow genuine consultation on matters of regional interest or vocational relevance.

Those who denounce the Faure reform 'which was to have been the renaissance of the French university' for having instead 'found itself distorted in the university's restoration to its former self' (Patterson, 1972, p. 281) may have initially had excessive expectations. They may be underrating the importance of political compromise and exaggerating that of purely formal provisions. Yet they also fail to acknowledge that any departure from the Napoleonic pattern could only be gradual, if only because of the academics' own dependence on it. In Bourdieu's words (all the more interesting since they were first published in 1967), 'the educational system . . . is deeply marked by its particular history and capable of moulding the minds of those who are taught and those who teach both through the content and spirit of the culture that it conveys and through the methods by which it conveys it' (Bourdieu, 1971, p. 204). They may have given insufficient attention to financial pressures. In a period of economic recession the shortage of funds has greatly undermined the new universities' ability to use their limited autonomy for innovatory purposes. Multi-disciplinary experimentation has been hampered, and governmental stringency, by stimulating violent political protest among students and sections of the staff, has destroyed the prospects of participation. Conjunctural factors have thus impeded the slow attempts at implementation of the principles central to the Faure reform. In addition, a major structural constraint was not taken into account by the *loi d'orientation*, and this failure to tackle the problem of selection can be seen, after a decade, to have been its major, perhaps its fatal, weakness. Conceivably, a complementary *loi d'orientation de l'enseignement secondaire*, contemplated by de Gaulle in 1969 (*Le Monde*, 30 March 1978) would have helped to solve the issue of selection.

SELECTION BY SHIPWRECK, OR THE SHIPWRECK OF SELECTION?

It was well known before 1968 that the main pressure on the university system was the increase in student enrolments, which doubled between 1960 and 1965 and trebled between 1960 and 1970.* The origin of this inflationary demand for higher education can be traced to the fact that the *baccalauréat* entails the right to register as an undergraduate – in other words, to the Napoleonic symbiosis between *lycées* and university: hence the need to eliminate large numbers of first-year students by examinations in order to prevent the 'clogging up' of the whole system and to avoid a devaluation of the qualifications offered, as well as of the standards applied. The outcome was generalized anxiety and an abnormally high ratio of failures. Minister Fouchet described this mode of assessment as 'organizing a shipwreck to see who could swim'. In 1968–9, out of 200,000 students registered in *lettres et sciences humaines* in France, 60,000 were in the first year. Statistics show that one student out of three entering a university did not even attempt the first-year examination; another one gave up at the end of the second year; and only the remaining one, having completed the first cycle of studies, could actually register for the second and work towards a *licence*. It is therefore understandable that the first cycle should have been resented as a burden by the staff and as a blind alley by countless students. Since selection at entry into the university was not a politically acceptable solution, because of its anti-democratic overtones, the only alternative was to screen students at various levels within higher education, in order to avoid the wastage prevailing since the Second World War, especially in the sixties. The use of examinations for purposes of rejection at the end of the first cycle would then be replaced by the establishment of graded diplomas and degrees, which could either be terminal or, depending on the aptitude shown and the results gained, could lead up to further levels of

*Hence the need constantly to create new universities. There will be seventy-seven in 1978–9, plus four university colleges (two of them overseas).

study. The Faure reform left this crucial decision aside and, by implication, shifted the responsibility for matters of assessment onto the emerging UERs.

Political pressures within the new units favoured continuous assessment. Yet, while the ideology of 1968 had been wholly hostile to examinations and, indeed, to the whole process of ranking and exclusion inseparable from the Napoleonic tradition, the student population, no less than their families, continued to display a marked attachment to formal qualifications. This attitude was a natural outcome of occupational concerns, as the labour market could not absorb all the trained manpower, certainly not in the type of posts that earlier generations of graduates had filled. Less natural was the expectation that failure could no longer occur and that some qualification would be ultimately secured as of right, provided enough time had been spent within the system of higher education. When selection becomes a kind of endurance test, failure may be precluded but success is devalued:

> As an adjunct to the Immaculate Conception of students, the system of the diploma by divine right asserted itself unobtrusively, but on a big scale: any individual whose family can afford to keep him in secondary education is entitled to the *baccalauréat*; any holder of the *baccalauréat* who does not need to earn his living immediately is entitled to a higher degree. (*Le Monde*, 14 April 1970).

In fact, the mystique of the *baccalauréat* as an entitlement to undergraduate status and that of the diploma secured by divine right (or, more prosaically, by mere persistence, without any tough form of assessment) both favour the financially secure middle class. Their offspring can afford the lengthy process of secondary and higher education, despite the adjunction of additional years. They are also better able than the remainder of their contemporaries to secure employment through a network of connections or by acquiring supplementary qualifications; for instance, by taking a course at a foreign university. If selection by merit recedes, social selection gains thereby − even though the former meritocracy implied elements of social selection.

The lack of a selection strategy at the time of the Faure reform has inevitably led to a perpetuation of the failure rate within the first cycle, evaluated at 50 per cent in 1976 by J. L. Quermonne, when he resigned from the *Direction des Enseignements Supérieurs* in the Ministry of Education. He pointed out that the first cycle lacked sufficient autonomy within the new universities (due to the specialized or 'vertical' lines along which the UERs had split). Denouncing the continuous state of uncertainty about their own future to which undergraduates were sentenced for a period of two years, he compared their status with that of the unemployed, whose ranks they were only too likely to join after giving up or failing. 'They have no status within the university . . . The first cycles are communities characterized by imbalance' (Quermonne, 1976, p. 4). The political repercussions of this generalized anxiety have been only too obvious. Its social implications have been to reinforce the advantages of the privileged and to dissuade the majority of the corresponding age group to register in higher education, even when qualified to do so. The failure to adopt an explicit selection policy at the national level, while qualifications remain state-recognized and therefore national, has shifted the burden of decision-making on to individuals and their families. The fear of failure, enhanced by the expectation of a high failure rate, is most acutely experienced by those who are least socially secure. Parental resources and/or previous acquaintance with the educational system act as buffers against the prospect of rejection. The offspring of the under-privileged are the first to give up in this race, since they are aware that they have few assets and are pressed to take up gainful employment as early as possible. 'Thus educational democratization is self-contradictory, generating consequences diametrically opposed to those which were intended' (*des effets pervers*) (*Le Monde*, 3 December 1977). The so-called 'perversity' of individual decisions, contradicting the planned effects of social reform, particularly in the sphere of education, is Raymond Boudon's version of 'unintended consequences' (Boudon, 1977). He does not attribute the failure of equalization to ideological and repressive factors, but to the disbelief in equality exhibited by the people concerned. Thus they either manipulate the system to their own advantage, or they give up if they do not feel capable of doing so. Their individual strategy is largely shaped by their earlier educational experience, and so are the expectations of their family. Significantly, the influence of the educational system is the greatest on those who are least able to take a critical view of assessment throughout the period of school attendance. 'Families are all the more convinced . . . that personal aptitude and merit alone account for educational success – rather than the social milieu – that they are more culturally deprived and hence more directly exposed to the adverse effects of their social environment' wrote Bourdieu (*Le Monde*, 11 October 1977). The absence of a governmental decision on selection by merit (that is, on the status of the *baccalauréat*) can thus be construed as resulting either unintentionally or deliberately from an acceptance of the *de facto* selection effected by the applicants themselves. Those who do not attempt either to enter high education or to comply with its requirements for assessment by examination, or those who prove incapable of coming up to the examination standards, are left to their own devices. Consequently, the function of pre-selection incumbent on secondary education has not been taken into account by the *loi d'orientation*, and Fouchet's shipwreck did not end after the events of 1968.

Under Pompidou's presidency, in 1974, an attempt was made by the Minister of Education, Fontanet, to turn the *baccalauréat* into a terminal degree, but the proposed reform was shelved with the arrival of a new administration. The incoming Minister, René Haby, planned a reform affecting selection throughout the educational system, including primary and secondary schooling. Its adoption by Parliament in July 1975 was denounced by opponents as generalizing the system of competitive examination by applying it to entry into the universities. The schedule for its implementation provides for it to be operational at all levels in 1981, after having been introduced in 1977. Being an economist, M. Fontanet had intended to adapt the school to the requirements of the labour market by channelling pupils into alternative routes (*filières*), either academic or vocational. M. Haby, who since the mid-sixties had justified his commitment to the diversification of secondary on pedagogical grounds, took into account mainly psychological concepts such as mental age and educability. The spirit of his reform was to work from the kindergarten (*école maternelle*) upwards rather than from the *baccalauréat* downwards. Its method was to multiply the transition phases (*charnières*) by setting up, at the beginning of the primary (lengthened by one year) and the secondary cycles, forms which would give support to the slow developers. Meanwhile their more mature or better endowed contemporaries could move on to the next year's course. The Minister's own description of his educational philosophy as 'liberal' tallies with this acceptance of 'natural' selection throughout the school system. It entails the exclusion of rigid selection mechanisms, segregating pupils into administratively defined categories with which predetermined percentages of each cohort are designed to fit. As will be argued in the following chapter, the outcome of his approach would necessarily be – if the reform remained operational for a sufficient number of years – to perpetuate inequalities of merit which are largely the product of the socio-economic environment. While the Gaullist reforms of the sixties aimed at adapting the meritocracy to modern technological society by increasing vocationalism, the Haby reform exhibits a much greater reliance on *laissez-faire*. In time this would lead to the 'self-selection' throughout the school of an academic elite and of other streams corresponding to other strata of the social hierarchy. 'With M. Haby, Giscardian liberalism has found its educational expert' (*Le Monde*, 13 December 1974).

In the medium term it is, of course, a political issue whether this educational philosophy can prevail, despite the opposition of the left and the resistance of the staff, represented by their unions,* to its implementation within the different levels of the

---

*CFDT, *Syndicalisme Hebdo*, No. 1670, 15 September 1977, p. 19, denounces the staffing, timetabling, programmes, textbooks and support procedures for the less able as discriminatory.

school system. In the short term the hope felt by most university chairmen and by the supporters of a *numerus clausus* for higher education that the secondary system would act as a filter, in accordance with the Fontanet project, has proved short-lived. Consequently, a bottom-heavy first cycle leading to a vocationally irrelevant *diplôme d'études universitaires générales* (DEUG) in law, science and the humanities has been considered by few employers only as a terminal qualification. It has inexorably generated an overspill into the further year leading up to the *licence* and the next two culminating in the *maîtrise*. Hence the multiplication of graduates in a period of rising unemployment in the mid-seventies. The inability of the educational system to absorb all those qualified to teach by virtue of the *maîtrise* was the unavoidable outcome of declining demand related to a reduction in the size of the age group requiring secondary tuition (see Norvez, 1978). No less inexorably did it lead to undergraduate restlessness by 1975, when a new student revolt threatened. The appointment of a Secretary of State, Jean-Pierre Soisson, responsible for reforming the second cycle of university studies and adapting the *maîtrise* to employers' considerata, marked a return to the Gaullist trust in vocationalism as a device for modernization. His successor, Madame Saunier-Seité,† who has attempted to foist the reform on reluctant universities and rebellious students, has had to answer cirticisms about the lack of consultation and consequent threats of alternative *maîtrises* designed by academics and students without reference to the *patronat*. Student strikes against both the risk of unemployment and that of employment in a capitalist framework has turned the crisis of the universities into a national debate all over again (Bienaymé, 1978, p. 31). This crisis is clearly a by-product of the difficulties experienced by university graduates in securing jobs. It is undoubtedly compounded by the successful competition of the alumni of *grandes écoles* on the employment market.

†Appointed Minister for the Universities in January 1978 and confirmed in this post after the elections.

MALTHUSIANISM AND MERITOCRACY

The network of *grandes écoles*, unaffected by the Faure reform, remains a Napoleonic enclave in an allegedly modernizing educational system.* Hence it perpetuates the blend of vocationalism with a meritocracy justified by its intrinsic attributes rather than by mere efficiency. Their reconciliation is effected through the device of the *concours*, 'democratic as a means of selection and elitist as a method of classification' (Vaughan, 1969, p. 75). The success of this pattern, after the defeat of 1870, when the *Ecole des Sciences Morales et Politiques* (the future *Sciences Po*) was founded in 1872, and after the Second World War, when the *Ecole Nationale d'Administration* was created (see Chapter 4), reinforced both the planned effects and the unintended consequences of the training it entailed. In other terms, 'the selection procedure increasingly became a means of recognition and confirmation, perpetuating an elite, rather than a rational choice of individuals ensuring the efficiency of cadres' (Vaughan, 1969, p. 102). Hence the *esprit de corps*, initially conceived as an outcome of meritocratic selection, has become the cement of a self-reproducing administrative class and the guarantor rather than the seal of vocational relevance.

The restlessness experienced throughout the educational system had a minimal impact on the *grandes écoles* after 1968. The special preparatory courses for the entry *concours*, organized in the *lycées* under the slang name of *khâgne* in the *Ecole Normale Supérieure* and of *taupe* in other institutions, had already been acknowledged by the Fouchet reforms as equivalent to the first cycle of higher education in the *facultés*. It was not an over-generous concession to those who fail after undergoing *'l'enfer préparationnaire'*, the toughest of training periods faced for two to three years by some 38,000 pupils and

---

*The term *grandes écoles* has never been defined. Some 150 establishments, with about 35,000 students, can claim the title of *grandes écoles*. A further twenty, mainly in business management, are known as such and train about 8000 students (*Le Monde*, 11 May 1978).

entailing up to eighty hours work a week. Such preparation can only be achieved by the exclusion of any personal life, whether defined as partaking of the pleasures common to their contemporaries, as keeping up with hobbies, as enjoying breaks or even as experiencing any solidarity with fellow sufferers. The whole system is designed to maximize competitiveness (*Le Monde*, 18 May 1977) among those who are capable of facing it – and two-thirds of the candidates have been prepared for it by their families from early childhood onwards. Since the number of preparatory forms is limited, mainly to the most renowned Parisian *lycées*, access to them implies an 'insidious selection', 'because recommendations count . . . i.e. some applicants are favoured because of their family background, with the sons of academics being given more favourable treatment than those of the 'powerful' (*Le Monde*, 10 October 1974). The less well-known but more vocationally relevant *grandes écoles* often remain fee-paying, so that selection by wealth applies.

Not only are the criteria of selection biased in favour of the privileged. Its outcome – secure employment for the alumni of the lesser *écoles* and careers with unlimited prospects in the civil service and the private sector for the most successful at the *concours de sortie* of the best-known ones – is not fully adapted to the requirements of modern technocracy. Elite cohesion is assured; the development of top-level research is not, since the doctorate remains a preserve of the university system and since the teaching programmes of the *grandes écoles* tend to remain static. The reform of the *Polytechnique* curricula in 1969, intended to stimulate scientific rather than managerial orientation, the growing co-operation between the *Ecole Normale* and some of the new Paris universities, or that between the *Ecole Supérieure d'Electricité* and Paris–Orsay, are instances of planned, government-supported change. The socialist proposal that all *grandes écoles* be placed under the jurisdiction of the Ministry of Education rather than run by specialized ministries is intended to bring them 'closer' to universities without integrating them. Restlessness in the schools, particularly the resistance to military status as the Polytechnique in 1977–8, is also a symptom of pressures for modernization within this privileged sector, rather than for its abolition.

The *grandes écoles* are becoming somewhat less remote from the universities, at least from some of the most sought-after establishments in Paris, where students rush to register in early July for the following academic year and where what has been called *'sélection par le sprint'* (first come, first served) operates (*Le Monde*, 17–18 July 1977, and 19 August 1977). Attempts have been made to widen the pool from which *grandes écoles* entrants are drawn, by introducing the preparatory syllabuses into the first cycle of higher education, for example, rather than maintaining the present monopoly of 'super-sixth forms' in a few Parisian *lycées*. However, they will not lead to genuine democratization while an informal hierarchy prevails among the new universities. Governmental attempts to compete by creating technological universities (for instance, in Compiègne in 1973) and thus 'to open a large breach in the traditional division of labour between the universities and the *grandes écoles*, the former specializing in pure advanced research, the latter in professional training' (Fomerand, 1977, p. 102) may well be logical as an implementation of vocationalism. Yet they are neither assured of proving successful, as the earlier experiment of the *instituts nationaux des sciences appliquées* has shown, nor could their success be achieved without introducing selection mechanisms. Indeed, the very existence of selection – even on fairly crude grounds – is a prerequisite for popularity, both with future employers and, for this very reason, with applicants. The search for security entails the rush towards selective entry, 'a rush towards anything that resembles a strait gate' (*Le Monde*, 10 October 1974).

Official statements stress that enrolments into the university system are not excessive (they correspond to 20 per cent of the appropriate age group as against 50 per cent in the USA and 32 per cent in the Soviet Union: *Le Monde*, 22 October 1977) and need only to be redistributed by an 'orientation' of entrants more appropriate to economic needs. Yet it seems obvious that the young are already guided by a concern for vocational relevance in their choice both of institutions and of subject matters. Hence the durable popularity of the *grandes écoles* and the growing relinquishment of arts courses (the decrease of *littéraires* was 3 per cent in 1976–7 and 6 per cent 1977–8 in relation to the year before, while the corresponding increase was 9 per cent in the sciences, 4.5 per cent in economics and 27 per cent in the new *filière* in economic and social administration). The only form of vocational training within the university system for which the government gave way to corporate pressures and introduced a *numerus clausus* in 1971, medicine, has retained a tough policy of highly competitive selection at the end of the first year: hence fluctuations in student enrolments – an increase in 1976–7 of over 1 per cent and a fall of 7.5 per cent in 1977–8 in relation to the previous year – and a corresponding growth in pharmacy (7 per cent in 1977–8) as a safer and related alternative specialism. The deliberate limiting of access to university entry remains an exception, but the strategies developed by potential applicants to cope with this policy may lead to further restrictions, particularly in dentistry. The temptation to make numerical cuts in order to save on university budgets, to reduce the impact of student protest and to minimize the chances of graduate unemployment must be strong for a government whose political support does not originate in the academic world and whose approach to vocationalism could be summarized as denouncing the contribution of the educational system to unemployment through the provision of over-qualified manpower. The problem of *surqualification* (Prieur, 1977) could thus be solved by a return to the Napoleonic emphasis on training. This could be dispensed either in *grandes écoles*, or in private establishments, or in a few dependable sections of the university system, the remainder of which would be marginal in terms of employment prospects and therefore of national investment. This 'marginalization' of the university system, denounced by the left as 'a plan promoted by Malthusian logic' (*Le Monde*, 13–14 November 1977), appears to be a logical outcome of the distrust in which it has been held, especially since 1968, by the conservative elements among the *patronat* and the bureaucracy. The current official policy – announced in the *Programme de Blois* before the 1978 elections – aims at doubling the intake of the *grandes écoles* over the next five years. Yet it is doubtful whether this target could be reached without some devaluation of the qualifications they dispense. More might not necessarily mean worse, but it would unavoidably mean less privileged.

The key issue of selection remains inextricably bound up with the stratification of establishments into unequal categories and with disparities between the policies of establishments officially defined as pertaining to the same type. The coexistence of *grandes écoles* and universities, the varying degrees of openness at entry into universities and the attractiveness of the so-called *filières nobles* (as contrasted with the devalued arts subjects) all bear witness to the pervasiveness of institutionalized inequalities. Educational selection confirms and legitimates existing economic and social hierarchies by giving to the privileged a meritocratic veneer acknowledged by the majority as a corollary of individual merit, while providing a ground for making such privilege hereditary. The whole sociological school surrounding Pierre Bourdieu has contributed to the demonstration, attempted in *Les Héritiers* in 1964, of the inegalitarian bias implicit in the concept of culture as imparted by any educational system. 'The school's function is not merely to sanction the *distinction* – in both senses of the word – of the educated classes. The culture that the university system imparts separates those receiving it from the rest of society by a whole series of systematic differences' (Bourdieu, 1971, p. 204). The more 'functional' an establishment, and hence the more extensive the differences introduced between its *anciens élèves* and other graduates, the likelier it is to produce a widely acknowledged elite. Malthusianism and meritocracy appear inseparable, whether among Chinese mandarins or modern technocrats, and equally reflective of the social inequality they buttress.

BIBLIOGRAPHY

ARCHER, M. S. (1977) 'Education', in J. E. Flower (ed), *France Today*, 3rd edn (London: Methuen).

ARCHER, M. S. (1979) *Social Origins of Educational Systems* (London: Sage).

ARON, R. (1976) *Plaidoyer pour l'Europe décadente* (Paris: Laffont).

BIENAYME, A. (1978) *Systems of Higher Education: France* (New York: International Council for Educational Development).

BOUDON, R. (1977) *Effets pervers et ordre social* (Paris: PUF).

BOURDIEU, P. (1971) 'Systems of Education and Systems of Thought', in M. F. D. Young (ed), *Knowledge and Control*, (London: Collier–Macmillan).

BOURRICAUD, F. (1977) *La Réforme Universitaire en France et ses Déboires* (Amsterdam: Foundation Européenne de la Culture).

DUVERGER, M. (1977) *L'autre côté des choses* (Paris: Michel).

FOMERAND, J. (1977) 'The French University: What Happened after the Revolution?', *Higher Education*, 6 (1), 93–116.

FRASER, W. R. (1963) *Education and Society in Modern France* (London: Routledge and Kegan Paul).

GOBLOT, E. (1925) *La barrière et le niveau* (Paris: Alcan).

MORAZE, C. (1966) *The Triumph of the Middle Classes* (London: Weidenfeld and Nicolson).

NORVEZ, A. (1978) *Le corps enseignant et l'évolution démographique. Effectifs des enseignants du second degré et besoins futurs*, Cahier no 82 (Paris: INED–PUF).

PATTERSON, M. (1972) 'French University Reform: Renaissance or Restoration?', *Comparative Education Review*, 16 (June), 281–302.

PRIEUR, J. (1977) 'Rapporteur' of the Commission Education du 7e Plan, *Le Monde*, 1–2 December.

PROST, A. (1968) *Histoire de l'Enseignement en France, 1800–1967* (Paris: A. Colin).

QUERMONNE, J. L. (1976) 'L'Université Abandonnée', *Le Monde de l'Education*, (October), 4–8.

RINGER, F. K. (1979) *Education and Society in Modern Europe* (Bloomington, Indiana: Indiana University Press).

SULEIMAN, E. N. (1978) *Elites in French Society: The Politics of Survival* (Princeton: Princeton University Press).

TOURAINE, A. *et al* (1978) *Lutte étudiante* (Paris: Seuil).

VAUGHAN, M. (1969) 'The *Grandes Ecoles*', in R. Wilkinson (ed.), *Governing Elites* (New York: Oxford University Press).

VAUGHAN, M. and ARCHER, M. S. (1971) *Social Conflict and Educational Change in England, and France: 1789–1848* (Cambridge: CUP).

ZELDIN, T. (1967) 'Higher Education in France, 1848–1940', in W. Laqueur and G. L. Mosse (eds.), *Education and Social Structure in the Twentieth Century*, (New York: Harper and Row).

CHAPTER 3

Social Stability and Educational Expansion

Michalina Vaughan

THE FALLACIES OF GROWTH

The contention of the previous chapter was that a succession of reforms failed to destroy the elitist bias of the French educational system, devised under Napoleon to produce a state-serving meritocracy. Yet, despite the survival of socially selective educational institutions at the higher level and of avenues leading up to them, the pressure of growing intakes might be expected to result in the democratization of outputs. Freedom of access to university for all holders of the *baccalauréat* has increased chances to gain qualifications. But it has also entailed a devaluation of degrees commensurate with the numerical increase of graduates and a diversification within the secondary and the tertiary system, intended to 'cool out' the excessive demands of families by channelling pupils into alternative establishments and/or courses. The politically motivated refusal to introduce an avowed selection policy regulating access to higher education has meant that social discrimination operates at an earlier stage of the individual's educational life. In other words, it is experienced at a time when the influence of the home, hence that of the social milieu, is stronger and more pre-

44

dictive of achievement than it might be after a longer exposure to the school system (Ringer, 1979, p. 187).

The alternative *filières*, or networks established to absorb educational demand, are rated according to their length rather than to the openings they offer in an occupational sense. The short, vocationally oriented *cursus* is systematically downgraded by applicants in relation to the 'noble' one, whose purpose is academic. Thus preferred networks are directed towards the perpetuation of the existing school system, rather than geared to the expansion of the economy. To this extent, the political design behind educational growth has been disproved in the sixties. Its assumed contribution to an increase in productivity has been eclipsed by its purely 'reproductive' function – that is, by its orientation towards the perpetuation of the existing teaching hierarchy. Among university students, only those who read law or economics appear to be intended for the economic system in general rather than for the staffing of the university system or the service of the state. This trend perpetuates the historical image of the faculties of arts and sciences as training grounds for future educators. It appears to have been intensified by the increase in the percentage of female students, traditionally attracted by the advantages of the teaching profession as an adjunct to family life. Thus both the effects of modernization and those of traditionalism have contributed to a discontinuity between educational output and the requirements of economic growth. The expectations with which the technologically oriented elite of the Fifth Republic* envisaged educational expansion have been proved unrealistic. They have been challenged by the inflow of entrants in the arts, science and, to a lesser extent, social science courses conducive to teaching careers. They have also clashed with the reluctance of academics specializing in these disciplines to train their students for the service of the capitalist society rather than for the disinterested pursuits of research and teaching. Freedom of

---

*This orientation reflects the education received in *grandes écoles*, particularly *Ecole Polytechnique*. On the extent to which *énarques* (ENA graduates) are seen as technocrats – see Chapter 4, pp. 70f.

choice at entry into higher education – with the exception of selective institutions endowed with special prestige – maximizes the lag between individual preferences and the needs of a modern economy. Vocationalism remains the antithesis of culture, according to academics, and the justification for setting up new (hence less highly esteemed) institutions, such as the institutes of technology (IUTs) established in 1965, or degrees, such as the *maîtrise* in 1967.

The other expectation attached to educational growth, that of an increasing diversification in the social origin of students, has also proved somewhat over-optimistic. Despite the steady increase in absolute numbers, from 74,000 students in 1936 to 130,000 in 1945, 367,000 in 1965 and 680,000 in 1971, their social backgrounds have not altered appreciably. The over-representation of the liberal professions and higher executives and the corresponding under-representation of the manual occupations (working-class children accounting only for 5.5 per cent of university enrollment in 1961, as against 58.5 per cent for the former group) endured. The size of the cohorts which attended school between 1952 and 1968 (that is, in the years corresponding to an increased post-war birthrate) meant that educational expansion did not have to entail a redistribution of opportunities. A ratio of 35 school-age children to 100 adults, compared with only 27 before and 24 just after the Second World War (INED, 1970, p. xxiii), meant that the traditional clientele of high education increased. Hence the democratization of intakes was slowed down by a constant mechanism of social selection. Graduates from a working-class background tend to be older than their privileged counterparts and to qualify for entry into lower rungs of the teaching profession, which are comparatively safe, if unglamorous. By contrast, the specialisms linked with economic growth, such as law, politics and economics, attract the children of employers and *cadres*, and new disciplines, such as sociology and psychology, have the most 'aristocratic' pattern of recruitment (*Le Monde*, 31 March 1970).

Despite the persistence of inequalities, which become most

obvious if the intake of higher education is analysed by reference to social origins, a degree of educational mobility has been a corollary of numerical expansion. Thus, roughly a third of *grandes écoles* students belong to the middle class, which includes medium- and low-ranking civil servants – a pattern of social ascension already established under the Third Republic. Educational opportunities increase gradually along a continuum of social gradations, as the studies conducted by Girard and his associates have shown in the sixties and early seventies: 'There is no break between two contrasting backgrounds, but a steady progression from the least well to the best situated' (Girard, 1961, p. 105). If this interpretation is accepted, a gradual improvement of opportunities appears to justify a qualified optimism about the prospects of the middle ranks. However, the pace remains sufficiently slow to warrant the bleak view taken of working-class and peasant mobility through education. Given the increase in graduate unemployment in the seventies, it is further doubtful whether the gaining of formal qualifications is truly conducive to occupational mobility. The devaluation of degrees due to the number of students and to the irrelevance of curricula to employers' demands – both of which are features inherited from the rigid Napoleonic system of education, with its emphasis on the *baccalauréat* – has not been remedied by the evolution of higher education since 1968. The lack of any mechanism adjusting supply and demand (whether by reliance on central planning, as in Eastern Europe, or on the market mechanisms, as in the United States) has resulted in an unregulated flow of entrants and graduates. Among them expectations are low, and passivity – opposed to the official ideology of participation – is on the increase. This attitude is a major obstacle to the attempts made since 1968 to modernize higher education and a stumbling block to its democratization. 'By an apparent paradox, it is precisely at the time when intellectuals are recruited from among wider sections of society (despite the persistent under-representation of the manual classes) that doubts are cast on the principle – rather than merely on the methods – of selection' (Vaughan, 1978, p. 189).

Among the multiple unintended consequences of expansion, the loss of status of its beneficiaries must be as bitterly resented as the narrowing of employment prospects within the executive/managerial range of posts which earlier generations of graduates confidently anticipated. The explanation of the 1968 events by reference to this double disappointment has been advanced by many qualified observers, including Raymond Aron, for example, and a similar interpretation may be made of student unrest in the seventies.

THE FAILURE OF ALTERNATIVE EDUCATIONAL PATHS

The counterpart of free entry into higher education and of its correlative expansion has been the need to generalize 'orientation' throughout the school system in order to cope with the development of parental demands for, and individual expectations from, education. The series of reforms of secondary schooling culminating in the Haby reform (see pp. 35–6), with its reorganization of the transition from primary to secondary, has been officially motivated by the need to impart a common tuition during at least one phase of the pupils' exposure to the educational system, namely the four years of the secondary first cycle, following five years of elementary education. However, despite lip-service to the ideology of *école unique*, the meaning given to comprehensivization has been mainly a regrouping of pupils belonging to the appropriate age group within the same institutions, the *collèges d'enseignement secondaire* (CESs), but without lowering the barriers between sections into which pupils are channelled by the 'orientation' procedure. Formal testing has been replaced by a more flexible formula, resting on continuous assessment by teachers throughout the child's period of school attendance. This change has been justified by the need to take account of differences in patterns of individual development and by the fallacy implicit in positing a mental age common to each cohort. Access to the *lycée*, now comprising only the last two forms before the *baccalauréat* (that is, the second cycle of secondary schooling), remains, in theory, available to late developers. Nevertheless, the initial orientation at the end of primary-school attentance appears to act as a self-fulfilling prophecy for the vast majority. Hence it is a crucial stage in each individual's career, not only within the educational system, but in terms of occupational prospects. The intake of the first secondary cycle is thus divided into roughly equal thirds, only one of which is intended to receive the so-called 'long' tuition in either classical or modern studies, leading up to the *baccalauréat*. Another third will be directed into the 'short' modern course, which, roughly speaking, replaces the former *collèges d'enseignement général* (CEGs) and represents a similar safety net for the less able pupils (who are generally those from lower social strata). The remaining third is the residual category of the least promising, the potential early leavers. Some of them receive primary vocational instruction (*primaire professionnel*) in terminal, transitional or 'practical' forms. Others are channelled into technical secondary establishments, the *collèges d'enseignement technique* (CETs). Finally, an increasing number leave the educational system at the age of 14 under apprenticeship schemes in accordance with the Royer law. This tripartite system reflects the distinction between intellectually demanding occupations, those which require practical skills and/or some manual dexterity only and an intermediary, somewhat elusive category corresponding to the growth of the tertiary sector in the economy. Its existence can thus be justified in vocational terms, provided the possibility of passage to a different stream or establishment is assured in individual cases to allow for differential rhythms of development. It is the contention of the Haby reform that a maximum degree of elasticity, with the multiplication of transitional forms and the possibility of remaining in the same form for periods of time adapted to the pupil's own pace, or of moving straight on to a higher form, ensures such a situation. Its opponents maintain that this apparent flexibility conceals a reliance on social determinism. They argue that individual orientation is a mere confirmation of the advantages or disadvantages acquired through domestic education and differential access to culture. Aptitudes considered as innate and used as yardsticks to allocate to the 'long' academic courses are in fact determined before the period of school attendance has even started. Thus academic segregation within the educational system is a consequence of social segregation.

Drawing the logical consequences of this challenge to the ideology of innate ability, sociologists of education have assessed critically the degree of coincidence between each *filière* or educational path at post-primary level and the social intake with which it is identified. Thus Baudelot and Establet (1974, pp. 82f.) have shown the extent to which the catchment area of the 'long secondary' coincides with the bourgeoisie and that to which its less gifted children have found a 'fall-back position' in the 'short secondary'. However, they have to acknowledge that the latter offers an avenue of educational promotion for 'the average pupils of the petty bourgeoisie' and 'the best elements of the proletariat'. Although it tends to be the network in which the failure rate is highest, and the average age in each form is greater than that in the equivalent form within its 'long' counterpart, it offers prospects of educational upgrading to approximately half of its entrants, who ultimately reach the *lycée* within two years of the *baccalauréat*. This success tends to be gained by members of the middle strata and has not in fact provided an effective means of promotion for the working class. It has, nevertheless, contributed to a measure of educational mobility, so that the part played by this *filière* cannot be described as wholly negative.

Some of the pessimism with which this *filière* is regarded results from the failure of the *école unique* to materialize within the CESs now attended by over 80 per cent of middle-school pupils, but rigidly streamed in 'networks'. Tripartite segregation takes the form of a subdivision into sections. The '*lycée*-type' section, for the best-endowed pupils, is characterized by a 'rationally devised curriculum' and recruits the highest qualified teachers specializing in one subject matter each. In the 'CEG-type' section, for the second-best, teachers offer at least two specialisms each and a pedagogical blend of subject- and pupil-centredness. Finally, in the 'transition' stream, one single teacher is responsible for the implementation of 'active' methods of tuition and is supposed to bring the least gifted up to the level of which they are individually capable (*Le Monde*, 9 September 1970). The elusive quality of the middle stream is obvious, as is the inverted ratio of teacher specialization and aptitude to pupil development: 'Whenever pupils are labelled as difficult to teach, [they are taught by] teachers who may be less well qualified, and who certainly have received a shorter training and are less well paid' (Snyders, 1976, p. 51). The failure of the CESs to redistribute educational opportunities is to a great extent the outcome of the teaching profession's reluctance to accept the implications of mass education. With a population of over four million pupils at secondary level (as against 300,000 before the Second World War), the equation of the teacher's role with the transmission of traditional culture is increasingly unrealistic, except perhaps in the academic stream. In the lower streams it is a remedial role which must be played. Although intellectually more challenging and more relevant to the needs of industrial society, it falls on the least qualified and least experienced teachers, often employed under temporary contracts and thus insecure about their future career.

The resistance of teachers' unions to the Haby reform, particularly to the *classes de transition*, has been expressed in egalitarian terminology, but the attitudes of the teaching profession to innovation have been tinged with conservatism. This stance is sometimes blamed on the increasing number of women, who made up two-thirds of the 500,000 teachers employed at the beginning of the 1977–8 school-year.* The dearth of male candidates has been related to urbanization and to the consequent disappearance of the village school master as a local notable.† The dissemination of information through the mass media and the earlier maturation of pupils have also detracted

---

*280,000 in primary schools and kindergartens, 190,000 in *lycées* and CESs and 42,000 in CETs.
†In the seventies, village schools have been closed at the average rate of 400 a year (*Le Monde*, 31 December 1977).

from the esteem in which the teaching profession was formerly held by a less sophisticated population. All these factors have contributed to the feminization of teaching, which in turn brings it into further disrepute as an occupational outlet. The social origins of many female teachers, the reasons for which they choose this career (for example, the convenience of long holidays in relation to running a home and raising a family) and their frequent lack of interest in political issues contrast with the traditional image of the *instituteur*. Such a background and such attitudes have been alleged to account for their acceptance of inequalities as natural rather than socially induced (*Le Monde*, 5 May 1977). The view that the school cannot be an effective agent of social change is commonly expressed when problems experienced by individual pupils are shifted away from the teaching situation by referal to a psychologist. The assumption is that each case should be examined in isolation rather than in a social context. The inadequate rewards of primary teachers have meant that what used to be a calling as well as an avenue of social promotion for the best pupils of elementary schools tends to be perceived now as merely a safe, if badly remunerated, position, without special attractions (*Le Monde*, 15 June 1977). As a result, the guidance given to primary-school leavers, which (in practice) determines the fate of most children, is often a mere recording of socio-cultural handicaps to which the school has offered no specific remedies.

However, survey results show that conservatism in educational matters is by no means the prerogative of either female or primary teachers. Although the sample investigated on behalf of *Le Monde de l'Education* in autumn 1977 included both primary and secondary teachers of both sexes, and although it was more radical than might have been expected (70 per cent intended to vote for leftist candidates, 18 per cent for the majority and the remainder for ecologists), there was a definite gap between the political and the pedagogical views expressed. Thus 40 per cent of the 620 teachers investigated favoured early streaming; 45 per cent approved of allowing pupils to leave school at 14 in accordance with the provisions of the *loi Royer*; and 57 per cent felt that pupils enjoyed a sufficient degree of freedom. 'There is a sharp contradiction between political attitudes oriented towards change and professional preferences for continuity' (*Le Monde*, 27 January 1978). It seems that the teaching profession, even if its members are more politicized and unionized than the remainder of the French population, is not prepared to adopt progressive attitudes in pedagogical matters. A commitment to social change is not synonymous with support for change within the educational system. Hence the decisions of left-wing teachers about the future of pupils belonging to underprivileged milieux may well reflect a strong commitment to the conventional (and conservative) definition of culture.

Parents may have a right to challenge decisions about their children's orientation, but the extent to which they avail themselves of this prerogative is predictably linked with their own socio-economic and, above all, educational background. The complexity of the system – which is hard for the majority of the population to understand, and which President Giscard d'Estaing is known to deplore – and the frequency of changes brought out by a succession of reforms under the Fifth Republic are bound to generate confusion. Hence it is difficult to foresee the impact of assessment at entry into the first secondary cycle, especially since subsequent reorientation is always considered possible.

At present, the French educational system resembles a huge railway junction: inter-city trains rush through at great speed, giving access to universities and *grandes écoles*; suburban trains get further from the main track and cannot hope to reach very remote destinations; local trains end up on sidings among wastelands. Yet everybody started out from the same station, without catching the same trains. It is dangerous to change trains during one's journey and it is often only at the end that one becomes aware of the direction one has followed, somewhat hastily, in the rush of the great departure. (*Le Monde*, 30 November 1977).

The parents' understanding of this initial choice and their ability to influence it favourably are determined by their own educational level, as are both their aspirations for their children's occupational future and the latter's prospects of educational success. Girard's studies, conducted over four years (under the auspices of the *Institut National d'Etudes Démographiques*) of a sample which reached the last year of primary schooling in July 1962 at different ages, demonstrate conclusively that, within the same income bracket, pupil achievement is closely correlated with the father's educational success, measured by length of schooling and diplomas obtained.

These findings amount to the recognition that education mirrors rather than transforms French society. At the end of primary schooling the intake of school classes faithfully reflects the composition of the active population, so that 60 per cent are children of manual workers, 27 per cent those of artisans, shopkeepers and employees and 13 per cent those of professionals. Five years later the offspring of manual workers comprise over three-quarters of early leavers, over two-thirds of the pupils of 'short' vocational courses and only two-fifths of those of the second ('long') secondary cycle, whereas the progeny of *cadres* accounts for 30 per cent of the *lycée* population. Thus, by a gradual process of elimination, the university comes to present 'the reverse image' of the active population (*Le Monde*, 2 July 1969).

The avowed purpose of the Haby reform has been to delay the operation of social determinism and to create a set of alternative, but inter-communicating, networks. For the reasons already discussed, the best and the worst achievers at primary level, who are respectively the youngest and the oldest primary leavers, are assured either of a *lycée* place or of ending in the technical sector, whether as apprentices or pupils. It is only in the case of those who are truly average in both age and performance that possibilities of upgrading exist – and these turn out to be subordinated to the socio-cultural status of the pupils' families. For the vast majority of each cohort a kind of 'negative orientation' results in entry into a *collège d'enseignement technique*, after a long period, in over half of the cases, in transitional or practical forms, and usually after poor perfor-

mance in all the subjects in the curriculum. Nor is their alloca-
tion the outcome of individual choice of a particular trade. The
scarcity of both information and actual places in the most
popular specialisms, such as electronics and telecommunica-
tions, means that pupils are distributed somewhat haphazardly
and that motivation is low. A sense of educational failure,
coupled with a distaste for manual labour which amounts to a
refusal of an unpromising occupational future (*Le Monde*,
14–15 March 1976), create mixed feelings of passivity and
rebellion within the CETs. Social origins are, predictably, very
unevenly represented within those establishments. In 1973–4
approximately half of their intake were the children of manual
workers, whereas those of professionals, *cadres* and industralists
accounted for only 2 per cent and those of middle-ranking
managers for 5 per cent, the remainder of their intakes being
accounted for by the petty bourgeoisie. The corresponding
proportions in the *lycée* were symmetrically reversed (25 per
cent, 17.7 per cent and 15.6 per cent).

The sense of aimlessness pervading the CETs – with their
high drop-out rate and the failure of diplomas, at a time of
widespread unemployment, to secure jobs – shows that (despite
all official statements to the contrary) no parity of esteem exists
between manual and non-manual activities. 'Like the ruling
classes of Ancient Greece,' wrote recteur Capelle, the
rapporteur of the *loi d'orientation* before the National
Assembly, 'the ambitious class which protects its children
against orientation towards technical education . . . postulates
that there will be a category of men who would no longer be
called slaves, but who are nonetheless bound to engage in
activities considered to be unacceptable for those who have
received our democratized education' (*Le Monde*, 1 August
1969). The almost complete overlap between underprivileged
social background and technical education is a measure of its
perceived inferiority. It is all the more striking that this
particular 'path' should have been followed in 1977 by an
increasing number of pupils. For the prestige of the establishments they attend to compare with that of the CESs, disparities

between the training and the status of teachers in both would have to be eliminated. Hence many vested interests hamper the reduction of lasting educational inequalities. The official reliance on multiplying apprenticeships (from 60,000 in 1976 to 80,000 in 1977 – *Le Monde*, 3 December 1977) in order to help the young overcome their employment problems, shows that alternative educational paths have proved ineffectual in the somewhat half-hearted attempt to bridge the gap between the training of future manual workers and the instruction of future non-manual workers.

THE FRAGILITY OF INSTITUTIONAL ARRANGEMENTS

This failure undoubtedly reflects the public's attachment to traditional forms and establishments within the educational system and its correlative distrust of new paths. An illustration is provided by the response with which 'short' higher education has been met since the *instituts universitaires de technologie* (IUTs) were created in 1966. In order to demonstrate the equivalence between networks, a 'long' technical secondary course has been provided and the *lycées techniques* have attracted a middle-class clientele. It is a logical development that post-secondary technical instruction should have been organized to compensate for the largely theoretical and, in the majority of cases, literary content of university education, as well as for its increasing duration (up to five or – given the failure rate – seven years after the *baccalauréat*). Considerations of economy, of vocationalism and of depoliticization prompted the organization of IUTs. These were intended to provide a two-year course, relevant to future employment in the secondary or the tertiary sector of the economy, for entrants who need only prove their aptitude for such training – that is, those for whom the baccalaureat is 'neither necessary nor sufficient' as a qualification (Boursin, 1970, p. 59). The Fifth Development Plan foresaw that 21 per cent of students in higher education would be enrolled in IUTs in 1973. Yet the whole intake of higher technical education, of which such establishments are only one part, accounted for only 7 per cent of this population in 1973. The shortfall has been explained by the ambiguity of this type of instruction, initially designed as terminal, but entitling graduates to enter the third year of university studies and therefore, some-what predictably, perceived as a mere introduction, incomplete in itself (*Le Monde*, 3–4 August 1969). Even after governmental optimism had receded somewhat, and after the expectation of 170,000 students in 1972–3 had been scaled down by the Sixth Plan to 67,000 in 1975–6, the actual number did not reach 44,000 (*Le Monde*, 5 October 1976).

The failure of the IUTs to attract a sufficient number of students to make adequate use of existing facilities and staff, let alone to warrant the promised growth, is thus obvious. It cannot be explained by objective disadvantages in relation to costs incurred and income secured as compared with those of their counterparts graduating from universities. However, it is the average who enjoy analogous rewards, whereas the most successful of university graduates are bound to secure better remunerated posts, endowed with higher prestige. Hence the explanation of the IUTs' relative unpopularity – despite the financial inducements, since over 40 per cent of their intake receive scholarships, as against a mere 17 per cent in traditional higher educational establishments (Boudon, Cibois and Lagneau, 1975) – can only be sought in individual strategies, intended to maximize potential future advantages. This interpretation is fully compatible with the finding that, in terms of social origins, the entrants of IUTs are not underprivileged by comparison with those of universities. Though their expectations are not very different, their assessment of their own potential induces a minority (roughly one in seven students) to opt for a course that can only result in keeping up with the average, not in competing with the best of graduates. A wider acceptance of the medium-grade positions offered in an industrial society would result in a greater inflow into the IUTs. Yet it is this acknowledgement of the limits placed on individual mobility by mass education and by a new division of labour that is lacking.

'Educational demand results from the aggregation of individual decisions independently arrived at and which thus have no reason to be regulated like Leibniz's clock to give the same reading as the social structure' (Boudon, 1977, p. 122). The unintended consequences of individual decisions, merely meant to maximize future assets, but disregarding the unlikelihood of the expected outcome in a context of massive educational growth, is to favour the traditional sector, represented by the universities and to jeopardize attempts at modernization through the provision of 'short' higher courses. It might be argued that their intake could come from lower social classes, whose expectations would not be as ambitious. However, children from such a background appear to be content with the instruction offered by technical *lycées* and to seek employment at an earlier age, whether under the pressure of economic necessity or because their realistic aspirations are geared to security rather than upward occupational mobility. Hence the IUTs suffer from a double competition in relation to two somewhat different catchment areas. In each case it is the conservative view that potential entrants have of the opportunity structure in the society in which they live that prompts them to apply elsewhere or to forego higher education altogether. Regardless of institutional reforms, social promotion remains perceived as the prerogative of those who have received an academic rather than a vocational education, and higher education as the preserve of the privileged. 'Objective conditions determine both aspirations and the extent to which these can be satisfied' (Bourdieu and Passeron, 1977, p. 248). Politically motivated decisions, such as the creation of IUTs (see *Le Monde*, 8 March 1972) cannot modify a structure of expectations rooted in the social structure itself.

It would be an oversimplification systematically to contrast the government's endorsement of modernism, equated with the vocational training necessary to an industrial society, and the reluctance of individuals to accept its implications for their own social position. Official policy may be rooted in attachment to a traditional stance on a historical issue, no longer perceived by the vast majority of the population as relevant to their current concerns. This is the case of the support given to denominational education under the Debré law of 1959. Catholic schools, through countless parliamentary debates about their status and financing, caused the division between secularists and clericalists to harden into one of the main political axes under the Third Republic. Their fate was still sufficiently controversial after the Second World War to disrupt the 'third force' majority which ruled the Fourth Republic. A major tenet of Gaullist policy, implemented by the 1959 law, was to acknowledge formally the coexistence of two educational systems, secular instruction under state auspices and a parallel network of denominational establishments. The state aid granted to them in order to cover staff salaries and some other expenditures entailed a correlative right of control proportional to the amount of this assistance. Changes within the Catholic Church have resulted in greater pedagogical liberalism, as well as in an inflow of practising Catholics into state schools, both as pupils and teachers. A redefinition of the political left as centring on social rather than religious issues has contributed to the weakening of anti-clericalism; so has the dwindling away of rural schools, with the attendant transformations in the teaching profession. Thus neither the clergy nor its traditional antagonists resemble their predecessors. The population of Church schools, which declined steadily through the sixties and rose only slightly after the disruption of 1968, remains below 20 per cent of primary intakes (Ardagh, 1977, p. 575). Contrasted with the pressing problems of educational inequalities with the state system, the existence of *l'enseignement libre* can be considered a historical residue and a potential source of much-needed diversity in a context of pervasive centralization. One is inclined to agree with M. Haby: 'It is not a real problem' (*Le Monde*, 15 January 1977).

Yet this non-problem appears to remain an electoral issue, as the reopening of the school war in 1977 demonstrated. While militant secularism seemed to be on the wane, except among teachers' unions, strongly represented within the Socialist Party, clericalism was one of the main common themes of a divided majority. It culminated in the Guermeur law of 1977, which granted to Catholic schools the building subsidies they had always previously been refused, as well as funds for the separate training of their own staff and the right for the religious hierarchy to control teachers' appointments. 'In order to defend educational pluralism, the Guermeur law introduces an irreversible educational dualism' (*Le Monde*, 26 October 1977). Paradoxically, the episcopate tends to stress change rather than continuity. It has argued that denominational schools are no longer clerical institutions; that they now involve secular members of the community, both teachers and parents, including non-believers, in their activities; and that they are less socially conservative than state schools (*Le Monde*, 18 June 1977).

Despite somewhat acrimonious controversies during a pre-electoral period, the former gulf between the two types of schools is being bridged. The staff of Catholic establishments is increasingly recruited from among the same social and educational milieux as those which provide the teachers of the state system, rather than from among the depleted membership of religious orders. Both categories of teachers are in the pay of the state, even if only one is in its employ. The ideological differences between them have largely receded, as has the uniformity of parental attitudes within each type of school. The major cleavages which accounted for the existence of secular and religious education as entirely separate and antagonistic entities, destined to inculcate incompatible philosophies and to implement different pedagogies, are largely superseded within modern French society. Extremists on both sides of the debate correspond to traditionalist enclaves whose attachment is to the past, whether to the militant secularism of the Third Republic or to the entrenched Catholicism of the pre-Council Church. The support given to denominational schools, even if it proves politically advantageous in the short term by embarrassing the opposition without alienating votes, is not an instance of far-sighted reform. Ultimately, the issue of autonomy is not limited to the denominational sector, concerns the whole evolution of education in France. The implications of growth, the discrepancy between centralism and the centrifugal tendencies at regional and local level (see Chapter 8), the earlier physical maturation of pupils and their greater intellectual sophistication, the changes in the prestige and in the ideology of the teaching profession and − to an extent that may have been exaggerated − the aftermath of the May events, all contribute towards a growing discontent with the rigidity and unwieldiness of state education. Sociologists have tended to focus on the compatibility of numerical expansion and the preservation of social inequalities within and through the educational system. Less attention has been paid to the incompatibility of the exigencies of growth and the demands (more pressing since 1968) for autonomy and self-determination. The somewhat formal participation of pupils' representatives and of parents in the frequently ineffectual *conseils d'administration* instituted by the Faure reform, does not satisfy either. Ultimately, the implementation of more egalitarian educational policies and of greater decentralization is subject to one precondition − the emergence of a wider consensus within French society about the purposes that education ought to serve as a guarantor of social stability and an avenue of social mobility. In the absence of such a consensus, governmental policy can only waver between over- and under-rating the attachment of individuals to traditional values: denominational schools and IUTs appear to be cases in point. Unlike the Third, the Fifth Republic lacks a consistent educational ideology and seems bent on pleasing some of the people nearly all of the time.

BIBLIOGRAPHY

ARDAGH, J. (1977) *The New France. A Society in Transition, 1945–1977*, 3rd edn (Harmondsworth: Penguin).

BAUDELOT, C. and ESTABLET, R. (1974) *L'école capitaliste en France* (Paris: Maspéro).

BOUDON, R., CIBOIS, P. and LAGNEAU, J. (1975) 'Enseignement supérieur court et pièges de l'action collective', *Revue française de Sociologie*, 16 (2) 159–188.

BOUDON, R. (1977) *Effets pervers et ordre social* (Paris: PUF).

BOURDIEU, P. and PASSERON, J. C. (1977) *Reproduction in Education, Society and Culture* (London: Sage).

BOURSIN, J. L. (1970) *Les instituts universitaires de technologie* (Paris: Bordas).

GIRARD, A. (1961) *La réussite sociale en France* (Paris: PUF).

INED (1970) *Population et l'Enseignement* (Paris: PUF).

RINGER, F. (1979) *Education and Society in Modern Europe* (Bloomington, Indiana: Indiana University Press).

SNYDERS, G. (1976) *Ecole, classe et lutte des classes* (Paris: PUF).

VAUGHAN, M. (1978) 'The Intellectuals', in S. Giner and M. S. Archer (eds), *Contemporary Europe: Social Structures and Cultural Patterns* (London: Routledge & Kegan Paul).

CHAPTER 4

The State Administration

Peta Sheriff

There is no better indication of the importance of the state administration* in France than the spate of criticism that it receives in the press and in a constant stream of academic and other publications; but then there must be few Western administrations that make quite so much difference to the daily lives of citizens. While the administration has always played a significant role in political decision-making in France, it appears to many current observers that this role has been aggrandized in the post-war period, reaching its culmination in the period of the Fifth Republic. This theme of the power of the administration is a central one in examining post-war developments; it is not only the extension of administrative power that must be considered, but also the repercussions of such power, for these can be viewed as constituting the most important administrative changes. To summarize very briefly the main argument of this chapter, France has witnessed post-war developments which have called into question the legitimacy of the extended power of

---

*'State administration' is employed here in the Anglo-Saxon sense of government bureaucracy at both the central and local levels. However, it should be noted that the French use of 'l'Etat' generally refers only to the central administration and its field services.

the State administration, and a new ideological justification for such power has been perpetrated which is expressed in official rhetoric and translated into new administrative structures and practices. This has taken place within the context of a strong administrative heritage which constrains the extent to which real change is possible. In the ensuing discussion the force of these historical constraints will be indicated.

THE NECESSITY FOR IDEOLOGICAL LEGITIMATION

The post-war administration in France shares with parallel institutions in other industrialized societies the marked phenomenon of the extension of its tasks. The change from '*l'Etat régulateur*' to '*l'Etat accélerateur du changement*' was a common modification in the post-war period, and the accentuated interventionist role of the state inevitably entailed a much wider range of powers and a much more signficant presence in a variety of areas, particularly social and economic (see Chapter 5). This was such a general phenomenon that it merits little comment; it merely serves as a reminder of the significant *quantitative* expansion of state activity and thus of administrative intervention.

Where the French administration differs from those of other industrialized countries in the post-war period is in having presided over a significant *qualitative* change in the administrative role in political decisions. In this context it should be remembered that the political and administrative spheres in France have never been as clearly separated as in the Anglo-Saxon tradition. Rather than maintaining the tradition of administrative neutrality and the consequent limitation on the political activities of civil servants, the French tradition has permitted, and even encouraged, its highly trained civil servants to serve the state in an alternative, political, capacity. This tradition has given rise to a set of regulations whereby movement from administrative to political posts is easily effected.* In a recent book tracing the composition of the 'French political class' from the 1830s to the present, Pierre Birnbaum mentions the varying proportions of former civil servants in diverse periods who have been deputies, oscillating between the remarkable proportion of over 60 per cent of the legislature during the rather unusual period of the July Monarchy to a modest 13 per cent in the period 1898–1940 (including teachers and professors, who are technically civil servants in France). Not only have former civil servants been active previously as deputies, but they have also played a key role as ministers. For example, 20 per cent of ministers of the period 1870 to 1940 were originally civil servants (Birnbaum, 1977, pp. 28 and 42–3).

Academic discussions of administrative power during the Fourth Republic are dominated by a consideration of the consequences of governmental instability for administrative initiative. The apparently logical link between the extreme impermanence of governments and the necessary extension of administrative initiative is a dangerous one, since the assumption that the permanent civil servants 'take over' to compensate for the lack of political initiative is not necessarily true. On this topic an eminent civil servant of the time, Francois Bloch-Laîné, writes (1976, p. 97): 'Undoubtedly directors, especially in the Ministry of Finance, have had more freedom of action, more personal influence, when ministers came and went, when governments changed often.' However, he admits that there were constraints on how far this independence could go without solid government support. The suspicion remains that the rather chaotic political situation of the Fourth Republic provided greater scope for administrative influence, at least in those ministries experiencing the most political instability.

---

*While the regulations differ slightly from one segment to another of the administration, the general rules are that a civil servant can easily take short-term leave for the electoral campaign and then, on taking up a mandate, is placed in a position of '*détachement*', retaining rights to promotion and retirement provisions during this period and to reintegration on return.

It is the Fifth rather than the Fourth Republic that is considered to have exaggerated this pattern of the blurring of the political and administrative spheres, and the arguments have nothing to do with political instability. One should note that Giscard d'Estaing is a former civil servant, and that all the prime ministers of the Fifth Republic have been drawn from the public service. Former civil servants have also been strongly represented as ministers (about 50 per cent of the Fifth Republic), though there is some recent information that the March 1977 cabinet reduced this tendency. Birnbaum provides evidence (1977, p. 71) that civil servants slightly increased their proportion in the legislature during the Fifth Republic to 24 per cent, but he emphasizes that higher civil servants tripled their representation between the Fourth and Fifth Republics. It is these kinds of data that have given rise to the popular designation of the Fifth Republic as 'le régime des fonctionnaires'.

But the political role of former civil servants is only the most obvious manifestation of administrative power. Even more significant is the role of serving civil servants in the state decision-making process. On this topic, certain provisions of the constitution of the Fifth Republic are frequently cited as greatly weakening the legislature, affirming executive dominance and thus facilitating administrative influence. The most obvious provisions are Article 34, which limits legislative action to certain specific areas; Article 37 which permits executive *ordonnances* and decrees in certain areas; and Article 38 which enables the government to request legislative permission to rule by *ordonnance* for a specific period of time in areas usually reserved for the legislature. It is argued that civil service drafts are much more likely to be modified through legislative rather than executive channels, and that the extension of executive power is diffused to the administration. What cannot be contested is that the constitution of the Fifth Republic provided for what has been called one of the weakest legislatures in the world (Suleiman, 1973, p. 749), and that at least one of the traditional controls over the administration has been diminished considerably in France.

The other constitutional provision (Article 23) that is significant is that membership of the government under the Fifth Republic is incompatible with a parliamentary mandate – at least technically. This has certainly facilitated the selection of ministers from among higher civil servants, as is reflected in the figures cited above; however, there was a growing tendency over the period of the Fifth Republic, under the strong influence of de Gaulle, to insist that potential ministers should first present themselves for a legislative mandate, and the proportion without such an initial mandate has decreased from 40 per cent in 1959 to none in 1969 (Vulliez, 1970, p. 30). Despite the resignation of their seats in the legislature, many ministers have retained at least one active foot in their 'constituencies' as an insurance for the future. But what is important is that the executive of the Fifth Republic is not technically an elected executive, and even if the practice belies the spirit of the constitutional provision, popular control over the executive, and thereby over the administration, is once more weakened.

Several other tendencies of the Fifth Republic appear to extend administrative power, including the increasing representation of higher civil servants in ministerial cabinets (now 90 per cent), those powerful advisory groups to ministers; the presence of higher civil servants at the head of new, powerful, parallel administrations (such as the *Commissariat du Plan*), which might well merit ministerial status; the extensive participation of civil servants in the myriad of committees, councils and commissions through which consultation with economic- and social-interest groups takes place; and the presence of former civil servants in important posts in the public and private sectors (Suleiman, 1974).

It is difficult to make systematic comparisons of administrative power in recent and earlier periods, for the whole topic is fraught with ambiguities and circumscribed by the impossibility of obtaining conclusive data. Yet there is strong evidence that both French and foreign observers perceive the administration in France as playing a forceful role in decision-making, and there is considerable concern that the post-war trend has been towards a continuing extension of, and emphasis on, such power (Debbasch, 1969).

ADMINISTRATIVE POWER AND IDEOLOGY

If administrative power is wielded in the name of 'the general interest', then it is almost sacrilegious to criticize the exercise of such power. As Suleiman has pointed out, the French administration has long occupied this 'sanctified' position, and the continuing force of this ideology is well illustrated by the views of administrators he interviewed, who are convinced that deputies, those representatives of a fraction of the nation, will always hold fragmentary views, while civil servants are the guardians of the general interest (Suleiman, 1973, p. 737).

However, it has been suggested that this ideology of the general interest has encountered considerable difficulties, culminating in the post-war period, and is experiencing a marked decline (see Chevallier, 1975 and 1976). The problems are ultimately related to the extension of administrative power, so that the direction of administrative intervention is much more visible; while it can be argued that economic development is in the interests of the nation, the idea that the interventionist administration is neutral and independent, equally accessible to various social demands, is much harder to maintain. Accordingly, while the ideology of the general interest, long forcefully perpetrated and diffused by public and private institutions in France, might still have a hold on individual civil servants, there has been a modification of the dominant ideology to allow for legitimate increased administrative power in the post-war period.

Two conceptions of the general-interest ideology can be distinguished. The first can be termed 'the Majestic State', according to which the state and its administrative apparatus maintain an independent kind of status *vis-à-vis* society and, through well trained, highly rational servants, are able to define which policies are in the best interests of the public welfare. This conception justifies a considerable distance between the administration and those administered, so that the state apparatus is not biased in its decisions by the influence of particular interests. The second conception can be viewed as 'the Negotiating State', according to which the state and its administrative arm are no longer, in a situation of increasing complexity, accorded the unique right to decide policies in the general interest, but rather act as arbitrators, who listen to the viewpoints of a variety of segments of society and, on the basis of this information, take a decision that reflects the interests of society as a whole. Rather than a marked distance between administration and those administered, this conception requires frequent contact between the administration and various segments of society in order that it may receive the relevant information.

But both these conceptions of the general interest require that the administration be subordinated to the political system, for it is through the processes of democracy and judicial review that society at large is able to initiate general policies and review specific decisions to ensure that it is indeed the general interest that is being served. When democratic control through a strong parliament and/or an elected executive is weakened, the notion that the administration necessarily acts in the general interest is more difficult to maintain. It is in such a situation that a new legitimation for extensive administrative power must be developed – and this new justification can be termed 'the Participative State'. This ideology requires continuing close contacts with those administered, but the spirit of the contacts must be modified; instead of seeking viewpoints or information, the administration must provide the opportunity for various segments of society to participate, in a democratic way, in the definition of desirable policies for society as a whole. In other words, the control that can no longer be guaranteed through the democratic process must be exercised in the very formulation of administrative policies.

One can suggest that the post-war period has witnessed a transition from 'the Negotiating State' to 'the Participative State'. In terms of concrete administrative changes, one could expect a gradual opening up of the administration to the environment, initially with a view to receiving information, but moving towards the encouragement of neglected sectors of society to have some degree of influence on decisions taken. If this is in fact true, administrative changes exhibit an ideological coherence which would explain the main important modifications of the post-war period.

The Democratization of the Administration: The Higher Administration

Among the most significant administrative reforms of the whole post-war period is the series of reforms which took place immediately after the war and which aimed to transform the structure of the higher civil service in particular. While the motives for the reforms might be phrased slightly differently in various versions, they comprise a strong emphasis on *democratization*, not only through recruitment, but also through the unification and standardization of the higher administration. The reforms included:

(1) the formation of a unified corps of civil administrators (excluding the *grands corps*)* to replace the previously fragmented structure in which higher civil servants were attached to individual ministries;

(2) the *Statut général des Fonctionnaires de l'Etat* of 1946, which aimed to standardize the conditions of service of the personnel of various ministries; and

(3) the setting up of *La Direction de la Fonction publique*, the approximate equivalent of a Civil Service Commission, which was charged with forecasting the needs of the service and with exerting a positive, generalized influence on personnel policy.

*The *grands corps* (*Inspection des Finances, Cour des Comptes, Conseil d'Etat, Corps diplomatique* and *Corps préfectoral*) are so termed because of their very high prestige and key functions in the French administration; they were excluded from the corps of civil administrators, ostensibly because of their long traditions and the specific functions that they fulfil, but perhaps because their suppression, even in the reforming context of the post-war period, would have been inconceivable. As we shall see, even now the *grands corps* continue to occupy a sacred position.

This unified context facilitated the key reform of the period, the foundation in 1945 of the *Ecole Nationale d'Administration* (ENA), the justly celebrated state training school for all higher civil servants in France (including the *grands corps*). The ENA was to be responsible for the recruitment of all higher civil servants and was intended to bring into the higher administration a much wider range of social, educational and geographical experience than had been the case previously. In addition, the ENA was designed to standardize, for the first time, the training experience of all higher civil servants and to complement their traditional legal training at the university level with exposure to the social sciences and to direct experience of administrative reality through a series of 'stages'.

In the over thirty years of its existence, it is undoubtedly true that the ENA has significantly marked the tenor of the higher administration in France. A new vocabulary has emerged – *'l'énarchie', 'l'énarque'* – to express the highly technocratic bent engendered by the school's training, and the graduates of the ENA are revered for their competence, though often criticized for their concern with form rather than content (see, for example, Mandrin, 1967). But it is still true that, in terms of democratization, the ENA has made little difference to the spectrum of social, educational and geographical experience brought into the higher civil service. Jean Luc Bodiguel, who has undertaken the most extensive study of this topic, concludes that the vast majority of ENA students are Parisian by schooling, if not by birth, are trained in law and at the Paris *Institut d'Etudes Politiques* and continue to come from the most privileged social backgrounds (1974, p. 244). In fact, he talks of a process of *'démocratisation à rebours'* (p. 241) since 1957–8. It is also worth noting that there is a high degree of 'auto-recruitment' through the ENA (that is, of children of civil servants), which makes for a closed universe. The final proof of the ENA's failure to widen the recruitment base of the higher administration is the recent official announcement that the Secretary of State for the Civil Service is currently studying reforms 'aimed at democratizing recruitment into this establishment' (*Le Monde*, 5 August

1977). But isn't this one of the objectives that the reformers of 1945 set themselves?

At least a partial explanation of this failure must be the exclusion of the *grands corps* from the unified corps of civil administrators. These prestigious corps, at the apex of the higher administration, have retained their traditional privileges: a higher salary because of various additional benefits and, particularly, the opportunity to occupy the key posts in the administration, the public sector generally and even the private sector, which guarantees a highly satisfying career for anyone able to enter such a corps. The attraction of these corps is such that entry to the ENA is a mighty scramble, occasionally attempted several times, and the battle to rank among the top 10 to 15 per cent in order to achieve entry to a *grand corps* continues throughout the school's programme. In effect, the attraction of the *grand corps* draws into the ENA the super-elite of the educational system who, because of the filtration effects by the educational system in the first place (see Chapters 2 and 3), are hardly likely to be drawn from a wide range of backgrounds.

Attempts, both official and unofficial, have been made to break this hold of the *grands corps*. Official attempts include the 1964 designation of the corps of civil administrators as another *grands corps* – but prestige and career opportunities do not necessarily follow on from official nomenclature. Potentially more effective was a movement on the part of the students themselves to break the traditional pattern. In 1972, in an unprecedented action, the most highly ranked ENA students insisted on ignoring the three most prestigious *grands corps* (*Inspection des Finances, Cour des Comptes and Conseil d'Etat*) in favour of the prefectoral corps and the traditionally denigrated social ministries. But their unusual action has not been sustained; subsequent cohorts have returned to the system whereby the traditional *grands corps* recruit the most highly ranked students, thus exaggerating the gap between these corps and the rest of the higher administration. This is one clear example of a strong tradition which has constrained the aims of a specific reform.

The continuing existence of the *grands corps* is only symbolic of a continuity of values in the higher administration; by leaving the *grands corps* in place, the reformers of 1945 indicated their admiration for the values that these corps represent: marked intellectual ability, as symbolized by the diplomas of the best institutions or, generally, an intellectual elitism. What the ENA has achieved is to have made the rest of the higher administration more like the *grands corps*, and the community of training has undoubtedly raised the level of the higher civil service. In this sense, the ENA truly reflects the values of the administration. But the school was given the impossible task of combining democratization with intellectual elitism; the former aim was specified, while the latter was symbolized by the practical reality of the *grands corps*. In this situation it is not surprising that tradition has triumphed over ideology and that the ENA has faithfully tended to homogenize the standards and recruitment patterns of the higher administration and those of the *grands corps*.

As to the content of its programme, certainly the ENA has widened the background training of the higher administration, although there is continuing criticism that the ENA tends to repeat the education provided at the university level, particularly at the *Institut d'Etudes Politiques*, and reforms being considered aim 'at giving a more concrete content to the course' (*Le Monde*, 5 August 1977). But the periods of direct experience of the administration and the private sector, and the efforts to deal with concrete administrative problems in the courses and seminars provided at the school, bear witness to a will to emphasize practical rather than theoretical training.

The standardization of the training programme has been less successful, and the ENA has had considerable difficulty in breaking with the specialist tradition of French administration. Despite attempts to organize a general programme, some degree of specialization – and thus of compartmentalization – has been reinstated since 1971.

The important structural reforms of the post-war period have clearly influenced the French administration over the past thirty years, but not wholly in the direction that the reformers anticipated. One cannot deny that the former extreme fragmentation of the higher administration has been reduced through common recruitment and a shared training programme, but some degree of democratization has yet to be achieved. The rest of the post-war period has been marked by continuing attempts to bring the administration into closer rapport with those administered, both through deconcentration* and through a variety of efforts to associate French citizens more closely with their much-criticized administration.

THE DECONCENTRATION OF THE ADMINISTRATION: LOCAL AND REGIONAL REFORMS

The simultaneous strengthening of the administration at both the local and the regional level may appear curious, but both sets of reforms can be considered within the same ideological context: 'meeting a genuine need of citizens who wish to be closer to decision-making centres' (Chirac, 1975). In the case of communes it was urgently necessary, as we shall see, that these administrative units, already almost too close to the people, should be strengthened in their ability to take decisions; in the case of regions there was a real concern to reduce the perceived distance between French citizens and the centralized decision-making centres.

The structure of French local government has been described as 'among the most irrational and archaic in the world' (Kesselman, 1970, p. 29); prior to the reforms of 1971 there were nearly 38,000 *communes* in France, of which several had ten inhabitants, half had fewer than 200 inhabitants and 90 per cent had fewer than 2000. France, with a population of 50 million, had as many local government units as her five original

*While various definitions of this term exist, I am employing it in the classic French legal sense of the transfer of the power of *execution* rather than the power of *decision* implied by decentralization. Abdel-Durand, 1968, p. 290.

Common Market partners combined, with a population of 130 million. The terms 'irrational and archaic' do not appear too strong. In such a context it is pertinent to ask why the structure of local government persisted.

Three main obstacles to change are highlighted:*

(1) social or traditional obstacles, rooted in a pattern of communal government established in 1789, which only slightly revised one dating from the Middle Ages;

(2) administrative obstacles, based on a symbiotic relationship between local notables and the departmental prefect (representing the central government), such that each side needed the other both to excuse errors† and to attain access to appropriate networks;

(3) political obstacles, despite recent trends, arising from 'the near deadlock between Gaullists holding national power, and their opponents who dominate local government' (Mawhood, 1972, p. 503), such that any centrally initiated change was suspected, perhaps with reason, of being to the benefit of Gaullists locally. In this context the apparently reasonable solution of a centrally dictated reform was much less reasonable in practice.

Accordingly, the 1971 reform was no authoritarian move, but rather a very curious and extremely interesting process of negotiation between *l'Etat* and local units. This was expressed by Pompidou in his Lyons speech of 30 October 1970 (quoted in Marcellin, 1972, p. 534): 'In a word, local democracy will have to be organized by relying on the free choice of local collectivities, a choice the state should guide and stimulate rather than arbitrarily impose.' Local opinion was consulted through the *Commission d'Elus*, with official assurance that even the

*This is based on Mawhood's (1972, pp. 502–3) outline, but many of the specific ideas come from others writing on French local government, particularly Kesselman (1970) and Grémion (1970a, 1970b). See also Grémion (1976).

†Crozier and Thoenig (1975, p. 16) quote one mayor as saying: 'State supervision (*la tutelle de l'Etat*) is not so bad after all. It enables me to be advised and, if I make a mistake, to be covered. I have no wish to be free.'

most archaic communal unit, embedded in an outdated rural context and inappropriate to the present century, would not be arbitrarily suppressed. Instead, the central government wished local collectivities to arrive voluntarily at some coherent plan that would be better adapted to local conditions.

Of course, the central government did not walk into the negotiation empty-handed. A wide spectrum of possible types of association between and among communes was one bargaining point. But as might be expected, the state's bargaining power was mainly financial, with assurances of a 50 per cent increase in equipment grants to the fused communes, financial assistance during a five-year period following the fusion and certain guarantees to locally employed personnel.

Despite such astute provisions, the reform of 1971 can be considered a dismal failure. As of 1 March 1975, there were 791 fusions, bringing the total number of communes down to 36,419. This failure arose perhaps because the communes were invited to 'commit harakiri'; certainly, the law was extremely permissive and put little direct pressure on local collectivities to be 'rationally coherent'. But one can also suggest that the traditional obstacles outlined above remain in place; in particular, as Grémion (1970a, p. 419) points out, 'the great majority of local elites are attached to centralization to the extent that their own power over local society is directly dependent upon it'; and they were the very people who were asked to recommend a strengthening of local decision-making. In such circumstances, and given the political opposition between the two levels, France seems to be wedged into these continuing archaic local structures. A change of power at the national level might help, but the complicity between local officials and local representatives of the central government would still have to be broken. In fact, one has the curious paradox in France that local power is sufficient to prevent a strengthening of local institutions, since such power derives from the maintenance of a centralized pattern.

As to regions,* the motive for their recent development was

---

*This section covers regional administrative structures; a broader discussion of regional policy and expenditures can be found in Chapter 8.

clearly expressed in 1969, when Philippe Malaud, Secretary of State for the Civil Service, wrote (with specific reference to the proposed regional reform): 'Attempts must be made to bring the centres of decision-making closer to the base ... only matters which truly belong at the governmental level should be channelled back to the central level' (Malaud, 1969, p. 11).

However, this motive of deconcentration was grafted on to an idea which had already had some currency in France as early as the nineteenth century, and whose territorial origins date back to the instigation of twenty economic regions in 1938 to facilitate the representation of regional interests to public authorities. Such consultation gradually developed over the post-war period and came to fruition in 1964 with the setting up of complex regional structures, including a regional prefect (in fact, one of the departmental prefects acting in this capacity) with a supporting mission, the Regional Administrative Conference grouping the various departmental prefects and several regional and departmental civil servants, and the Commission for Regional Economic Development (CODER). These CODERs grouped locally elected officials designated by the General Councils at the departmental level, representatives of professional organizations and other individuals designated by the Prime Minister. Their consultative powers concerning social and economic development and planning were expressed through the regional section of the plan. This structure has been termed a '*région de programme*' (Abdel-Durand, 1968, p. 14).

The regional concept was given a new impetus by de Gaulle in 1968, when he launched the idea of regionalization – that is, something *more* than a programming structure. Such a conception was certainly consistent with the development of the regional idea over time, but Legres (1975, p. 10) suggests that de Gaulle, with his uncanny political sense,* saw an answer to the 1968 spirit of protest in extended regionalization: 'The state had to be saved from itself by forcing decentralization on an

---

*One might add that this move was quite in keeping with a general post-war policy of containment through participation, as evidenced, for example, by developments in private industry (cf. Chapter 5).

administration driven to the edge of the abyss by the excess of its arrogance.' The referendum of 27 April 1969 put de Gaulle and an extended regionalization to the test, and both were narrowly defeated. It is, of course suggested that the defeat was a political one rather than a defeat of the concept of the regionalization of power; this interpretation would suggest that de Gaulle and Senate reform, both of which were linked to regionalization in the referendum, were defeated, but not necessarily the regional idea itself. Certainly, the referendum, if passed, would have made the regions 'into levels for the deconcentration of economic decisions, so as to relax the grip of central administrative organs' (le Débat régional, *Regards sur l'Actualité* 15 November 1975, p. 20). The Senate reform was designed to facilitate regional representation at the national level. What France in fact got was a much weakened version of such a conception through the regional reforms of 1972.

The present regional structure is little more than the 1964 version; it was conceived by Pompidou as 'expressing a consensus of the *départements* within it rather than imposing supervision upon these *départements*' (speech at Lyons, 30 October 1970; quoted in *Débats*). It consists, first of all, of a regional council, composed of all deputies and senators of the region, of representatives of the General Council of the departments, of municipal councils and of urban community councils, in which these various representatives equal the number of deputies and senators. Secondly, there is an economic and social committee consisting of representatives of interest groups (from trade unions to sports organizations) and individuals with particular qualifications. This committee must be consulted before the regional council votes any resolution. Then there is the regional prefect, as before, who must provide the region with necessary administrative services, and a continuation of the Regional Administrative Conference.

Most interesting is the size of the regional administrative budgets; these consist of the proceeds from the issue of all driving licences in the region, and there is the power to add a supplement to certain existing taxes, the total not to exceed 25 francs per capita per year in the post-1974 period. M. Peyrefitte has assured the people of France that: 'The region will only cost each of its inhabitants the price of a daily cigarette' (quoted in Merigot, 1974, p. 123); it is tempting to remark that one hopes that the value put on the regional structure is not similarly that of a daily Gauloise. But the budget symbolizes regional power in the area of economic and social development, which has been designated the main task of the regions.

Overall, there is some danger, at least in the short term, that the present structures will only accentuate the pattern of centralization that typifies France. There is, of course, the possibility of additional reforms with the agreement of all levels of government. The much-vaunted rhetoric in favour of deconcentration has given birth to weak administrative structures which were not intended to modify powers at the communal or departmental levels, but which, in fact, are unlikely to modify those of *l'Etat* either (Wright, 1974, and Wright and Machin, 1975).

PARTICIPATION IN THE ADMINISTRATION: ADMINISTRATORS AND CLIENTS

The cataclysmic events of May 1968 symbolized a major crisis in state/citizen relations; the usual stringent criticisms of the administration became more frequent and were acknowledged by ministers responsible for the administration. In 1969 Philippe Malaud wrote: 'To make the administration both humane and efficient is the aim of the reforms which the Prime Minister asked me to undertake' (p. 9), and the last decade has witnessed an emphasis on reforms designed to humanize and simplify the administration. This group of reforms includes disparate, and sometimes pathetic, attempts to gather information about how the administration is perceived by users, and to associate all citizens, whether employees or clients of the state, with the decision-making process.

In terms of *information*, the administration has always had available means of obtaining the views of citizens, including optional or obligatory opinion polls on various matters. But the past decade has been marked by a detailed attempt to obtain specific suggestions as to how the administration could provide a better service. Examples of such efforts include the so-called *missions d'observation* in the north and in Aquitaine of 1969–70, when two groups, mainly composed of civil servants, were given the task of finding out what criticisms were directed at the administration in these two representative regions. Similar in purpose, though more permanent in function, are the seventeen *comités d'usagers* in various ministries, which are also charged with the humanization of relations with administrative clients and which have emphasized the need for a simplification of administrative procedures and for a change in the spirit of the administration. It is tempting to be merely amused by these efforts, but they are undertaken in a spirit of tremendous seriousness, perhaps explained by the comment of the president of the *comités d'usagers*: 'Figuratively speaking, it could be said that the revolution, if there were to be one, would come from those administered rather than from producers or consumers' (Rolland, 1976, p. 90).

The *consultative* attitude, in the context not only of obtaining information, but also of associating administrators or clients at various stages of the decision-making process, has been present throughout the post-war period (cf. Langrod, 1972) and is perhaps best exemplified by the planning process and its host of associated consultative organs (see Chapter 5 for further details). The present ideological importance of consultation is indicated by an estimated nearly 5000 consultative committees at the national level alone. It is certain that the mere setting up of consultative organs is no guarantee that consultation will take place. At the individual level the link between consultation and perceived official 'irresponsibility' often leads to a singular lack of co-operation: 'Consultation . . . is all too often experienced by civil servants as an intrusion of outsiders into their preserve' (Aulagnon and Janicot, 1975, p. 315). Furthermore, certain powerful groups, notably business interests and organized pressure groups, dominate the process of consultation with the administration, and criteria other than those of democracy come into play as the administrators consult those whose views cannot be ignored for various reasons, or those whose views are most like their own and thus most comfortable to hear.

A major aspect of the debate on *participation* concerns the stage at which groups are consulted: that is, in the actual formulation of the decision, or at a stage when the decision has already been formulated and the contact takes on the aura of a mere formality. A concrete example comes from the recent experience of the *commissions administratives paritaires* (Ayoub, 1968), which group representatives of the administration and of employees in equal numbers and which were set up to deal with individual matters in the various relevant corps. Despite a strong legal framework, in which opinions are obligatorily required on matters of evaluation, advancement and discipline, the actual practice reveals that the prior preparation of relevant documents by the administration and their tardy communication to employees' representatives diminish considerably the influence of the latter group. This situation is exacerbated by the fact that the chair of each *commission* is taken by an administration representative who has the deciding vote, so that decisions are really settled in advance by the administration. Furthermore, decisions are not binding on the minister. Ayoub concludes that the influence of employees' representatives 'is rather restricted . . . In no way does it amount to a participation of workers in the management of the enterprise or to democratization of the French administration' (p. 703).

Couched in much more positive terms are reports of groups at the local level who are associated in the decision-making process. Thus accounts of the functioning of *groupes d'action municipale* (or citizens groups) in such local contexts as Caen, Grenoble and Vitry suggest that these recent spontaneous groupings have not yet experienced the process of institutionalization that diminishes enthusiasm and ideological purity; but even these local examples of participation, frequently focused on minor decisions, experience the usual difficulties in involving all social categories equally in the decision-making process.

A final type of participation is *protest*, and the administration has recently institutionalized a form of protest through the office of the *Médiateur* which symbolizes the participatory mentality of the recent decade in a particularly clear fashion. It is certain that the office was conceived as linking up 'with the group of reforms undertaken by the government over the past four years with the intention of bridging the gap between the administrator and the citizen' (Pleven, Minister of Justice, cited in Brown and Lavirotte, 1974, p. 212); it was also designed 'to remedy loss or injury sustained in the individual case and not to solve general problems or to start general reforms' (*ibid.*, p. 214). In fact, the evidence of the operation of the office would suggest that it is being used to solicit information from citizens, and the initial holder of the office certainly envisaged as one of his main tasks a contribution towards administrative reform (Pinay, 1973, p. 615).

The *Médiateur* is thus placed on the side of the administration, assisting it in reducing potential points of tension with citizens, but he is not placed firmly on the side of the citizens, representing their grievances to the administration. And, in general, one might suggest that the various participative measures have been imbued with this aura of extracting, by all possible means, sufficient information to manage the tension between the administration and the people of France.

The institution is still in its youth, and it is difficult to offer any judgement of its functioning. So far, the number of cases referred to the *Médiateur* have been fewer than the *Médiateur* himself would have liked, though perhaps average (per inhabitant) by comparison with the situation in other countries. However, as Lindon points out (1974, p. 2), a popular radio personality on Europe I who was concerned with citizens' complaints received fourteen times as many complaints against the public services as did the *Médiateur* in the first year of his functioning. Efforts are being made to publicize the office, which has been blessed with considerable public indifference since its institution.

In reviewing the various degrees of participation one gains the impression of an observance of the form of participation rather than of its spirit. Certainly, the events of May 1968 were a symbol of the crisis in the relationship between the state and French citizens, as mediated by the administration. This crisis has been taken seriously, but more at the rhetorical rather than the effective level. It is easy to find evidence in various official speeches of the will to bring the administration closer to those administered; it is much less easy to find direct evidence of a change in administrative practices in line with this ideology.

The evidence of the continuing force of the traditional administrative hierarchy is always present, symbolized best by the fact that the French *Médiateur*, ostensibly given the task of defending French citizens in their dealings with the administration, has assumed a reformist role on behalf of the administration. But if such institutionalized protest does not prove effective, will the citizens of France feel, once again, that direct protest is the only alternative?

The legacy of tradition dies hard. There is still a strong vestige of 'the Majestic State' in the attitudes of administrators: it is still apparent that they feel it is their duty to look after *La France* rather than *Les Français*, and that the sacred position of the administration requires an overall view, on which individual interests should not impinge. There is also a trace of the former ideology in the strong, continuing importance of the traditional hierarchy. In effect, the years of early socialization and the official training of administrators in an authoritarian and benevolent concern with the general interest of the nation will not be transformed immediately by official pronouncements, however politically advisable.

As to 'the Negotiating State', there is certainly the structural opportunity, through the numerous consultative committees and commissions, for certain selected groups outside the administration to express their views; however, the debates concerning the real impact of such information are not without importance. While the ideology would require a genuine concern with a balancing of a variety of viewpoints, it is just as easy for the consultative process to become a legitimation for decisions taken in advance. This may be a harsh judgement and, in many cases, external input into administrative decisions may well be taken into account, but, as we have seen, the selection of informants and the considerable administrative preparation prior to consultation often reduces the impact of those consulted.

Of all the ideologies, that of 'the Participative State' is by far the most ambitious. Democratic control through participation in decision-making is difficult to achieve in small, personalized organizations; how much greater the challenge in a vast, impersonal, state administration. Chevallier suggests that deconcentration has really facilitated greater centralization: the peripheral administrative units have limited powers; the intervention of centralized power continues, though perhaps in a slightly different way; and financial control remains in Paris (1976, pp. 120–1). In fact, the appearance of deconcentration has permitted a kind of recentralization; it is easy to justify the necessity for new and powerful co-ordinating agencies (the so-called *administrations de mission*) in order to render discrete and fragmentary measures coherent. Hence the proliferation of inter-ministerial missions, delegations and commissariats, which are theoretically temporary, designed to attack specific problems, but which, in practice, take on a life of their own and reinforce centralized decision-making through their access to a wide variety of sources of information. The structures for deconcentration exist, but it has been impossible to break the centralized pattern in which local power is embedded and to which it has become adapted.

The multiple consultative and participative structures at least serve one important purpose for the administration – that of obtaining information from those administered. Rather than a spirit of negotiation or participation, the state administration in France seems to have opted, in practice, for a spirit of prevention. The many sources of information can serve both to legitimate state action and to provide a warning of changes that must be undertaken if conflict is to be avoided. It is thus that the *Médiateur's* role becomes important, for this official can become a highly privileged source of information about possible difficulties between the administration and its clients. Similarly, the vast range of information that flows in through consultative bodies and peripheral units is a useful indication of what is politically advisable in terms of administrative reform. In practice, participative and consultative structures, whatever the rhetoric, are redirected to prevent future conflict between the administration and the citizens of France.

BIBLIOGRAPHY

ABDEL-DURAND, M. (1968) 'Région, déconcentration ou décentralisation', *Departements et Communes*, Sept.–Oct., 290–3.

AULAGNON, T. and JANICOT, D. (1975) 'La communication entre administration et administrés', *La Revue administrative*, 28 (165), 311–19.

AYOUB, E. (1968) 'Les commissions administratives paritaires', *La Revue administrative*, 21 (126), 700–3.

BIRNBAUM, P. (1977) *Les sommets de l'Etat* (Paris: Seuil).

BLOCH-LAINE, F. (1976) *Profession: fonctionnaire* (Paris: Seuil).

BODIGUEL, J. L. (1974) 'Sociologie des élèves de l'Ecole Nationale d'Administration', *International Review of Administrative Sciences*, XL (3), 230–44.

BROWN, L. N. and LAVIROTTE, P. (1974) 'The Mediator: A French Ombudsman?', *The Law Quarterly Review*, 90 (358), 211–33.

CHEVALLIER, J. (1975) 'L'intérêt général dans l'administration française', *Revue internationale des Sciences administratives*, 41 (4), 325–50.

CHEVALLIER, J. (1976) 'La participation dans l'administration française: discours et pratique', *Bulletin de l'Institut international d'Administration publique*, (37), Jan.–March, 85–119, and July–Sept., 85–142.

CROZIER, M. and THOENIG, J. C. (1975) 'La régulation des systèmes organisés complexes: le cas du système de décision politico-administratif local en France', *Revue française de Sociologie*, 16 (1), 3–32.

DEBBASCH, C. (1969) *L'Administration au Pouvoir* (Paris: Calmann-Lévy).

GREMION, P. (1970a) 'Réforme régionale et démocratie locale', *Projet*, 44, 411–29.

GREMION, P. (1970b) 'Introduction à une étude du système politico-administratif local', *Sociologie du Travail*, 12 (1), 51–73.

KESSELMAN, M. (1970) 'Overinstitutionalization and Political Constraint', *Comparative Politics*, 3 (1), 21–44.

LANGROD, G. (1972) *La consultation dans l'administration contemporaine* (Paris: Cujas).

LEGRES, J. (1975) 'Une certaine idée de l'Etat', *Etudes* (Paris), January, 5–14.

LINDON, R. (1974) 'L'ombudsman à la mode française – le Médiateur', *La Semaine juridique*, 48 (22), Doctrine 2634, 1–4.

MALAUD, P. (1969) 'Réformes dans l'administration française d'aujourd'hui', *Bulletin de l'Institut international d'Administration publique*, 9, 7–20.

MANDRIN, J. (1967) *L'énarchie ou les mandarins de la société bourgeoise* (Paris: La Table ronde de Combat).

MARCELLIN, R. (1972) 'La réforme communale en France', *Nouvelle Revue des deux Mondes*, 3, 519–34.

MAWHOOD, P. (1972) 'Melting an Iceberg: The Struggle to Reform Communal Government in France', *British Journal of Political Studies*, 2 (4), 501–9.

MERIGOT, J.-G. (1974) 'La région en vedette', *Défense nationale*, 30, 117–26.

PINAY, A. (1973) 'Quelques réflexions sur l'institution du médiateur', *La Revue administrative*, 26 (156), 615–19.

ROLLAND, H. (1976) 'L'amélioration des rapports entre administration et citoyens: les comités d'usagers', *Revue française du Marketing*, 60, 85–94.

SULEIMAN, E. (1973) 'L'administrateur et le député en France', *Revue française de Science politique*, 23 (4), 729–57.

SULEIMAN, E. (1974) *Politics, Power and Bureaucracy in France* (Princeton: Princeton University Press).

VULLIEZ, C. (1970) *Les grands corps de l'Etat: ceux qui restent quand le gouvernement change* (Paris: Dunod).

WRIGHT, V. (1974) 'Politics and administration under the French Fifth Republic', *Political Studies*, 22 (1), 44–65.

WRIGHT, V. and MACHIN, H. (1975) 'The French regional reforms of July, 1972: A case of disguised centralisation?', *Policy and Politics*, 3 (3), 3–23.

CHAPTER 5

Industry and Commerce: Problems of Modernization

Peta Sheriff

The industrial and commercial sector in France has experienced a major change in the post-war period, transforming the nation from an 'under-industrialized' country into a major indus-trailized nation of the 1970s. This economic growth has been accompanied by an important, though subtle, change in relationships among the three main economic actors – the state, businessmen and employees – such that the earlier paternalistic and archaic relations have apparently given way to a spirit of dialogue. In effect, French business has been hauled into the twentieth century in a short span of thirty years and has effected significant changes in many facets of its traditional mode of operation.

It should be recognized that there was considerable room for improvement in the immediate post-war economy, which has been termed 'exasperatingly mediocre'. The 1949 rate of industrial production was about the same as that of 1913 (*Expansion*, 1968, p. 111), and for the period 1929 to 1949 the average annual rate of growth of industrial production hovered around a meagre 1 per cent.* It is generally agreed that France

---

*Kaspereit, 1970, p. 188, gives the following average annual growth rates of industrial production in the first half of the twentieth century: 1896–1913 – 2.4 per cent; 1913–29 – 2.6 per cent; 1929–39 – 1.1 per cent; 1938 [sic]–49 – 0.8 per cent.

was considerably behind most other industrialized countries in the immediate post-war period – hence the description 'under-industrialized'. The explanations for such stagnation are varied: French capitalism, protected behind customs barriers and exchange controls, successively missed significant turning points in terms of technical advances (Hincker, 1967); the very slow rate of population growth over the first half of this century did not provide the natural dynamism of an increasing internal market and working population* (Sheahan, 1969, p. 3; Kaspereit, 1970, p. 189); excessive state intervention, or the wrong kind of intervention, made for a mediocre performance (Sheahan, 1969, pp. 21–2). But mentioned most often, perhaps, is the image of an archaic and denigrated French business class, which was wedded to stability, security and the advantages of the small or medium-sized firm.† It is suggested that French businessmen lacked an entrepreneurial spirit and, while occasional pioneers were produced, France had a great capacity for 'keeping these people in their place'. The traditional attitude towards exports was to send abroad the surplus from the internal market; the classic attitude towards expansion was negative, since it would have entailed the loss of control of the traditional family firm; and all should be allowed their place in the sun, including the smallest firm on the border of effective performance, since such firms provided an important avenue of upward mobility (cf. Landes, 1951; Sheahan, 1969, pp. 24–5; Kaspereit, 1970, p. 193). This latter point is important and is best expressed in a statement of the Radical and Radical–Socialist party of the early 1950s:

> This party does not conceal its preference for small and middle-sized undertakings . . . principally because they are an indispensable stage enabling workers and employees to throw

*The total population increased very slightly over the fifty-year period 1896–1946 from 38.6 million to 40.3 million (Kaspereit, 1970, p. 189), while the size of the working population hardly varied (McDowall, 1973, p. 4).
†It is interesting that a similar image of the Québecois businessman is put forward as an explanation for the relatively limited participation of francophones in the industrial development of their province (see Taylor, 1961).

off the yoke of wage-earning and attain proprietorship, and the conditions which shall permit the full development of their personalities. (Goertz-Girey, quoted in Chamberlin, 1954, p. 42)

This is a strong French tradition and goes some way towards explaining the continuing importance of small and medium-sized firms, even in the transformed post-war economy.

Against the backdrop of this dismal image, post-war progress takes on its full significance. The economy was able to experience 'a strongly sustained growth at an unprecedented pace' (Page, 1975, p. 9). For example, the average annual rate of growth of the GNP was 5.8 per cent over the period 1960–72, a rate that was not exceeded by that of any other Common Market country (Euvrard, 1975, p. 33)* and was exceeded internationally only by that of Japan. The average annual rate of growth in industrial production was 6.3 per cent for the years 1960–5 and 7.5 per cent for the period 1965–70 (Boulard, 1975, p. 112). Exports increased by between five and six times (depending on the yardstick used) between 1958 and 1972; the proportion of manufactured goods rose to dominate exports (51 per cent) by 1972; and France ranked fourth (after the United States, Germany and Japan) in the volume of goods exported by the same date (*Notes et Arguments*, 1973). For a country supposedly dominated by unenterprising businessmen, with a negative attitude towards exports as recently as the 1940s, this was a surprising transformation.

Economic explanations of this phenomenon abound; fre quently cited is an important work by Carré, Dubois and Malinvaud (1972), in which they attempt to distinguish the main factors that gave rise to general economic growth in France in the post-war period. They conclude that factors linked to work (some increase in the working population post-1962, internal migration from agriculture to industry and improvement in the 'quality' of work) can be considered to account for about 1 per cent of the economic growth over the 1950s and 1960s, and that

---

*The comparable rate for Great Britain in the same period was 2.7 per cent and for Germany, 4.5 per cent.

factors linked to capital (the volume of net capital and the renewal of capital stock) might account for another 1½ per cent of the growth in the same period. But such an analysis would still leave about half of the growth rate of the period unexplained (it is attributed to 'technical progress and various other factors'). While the economic explanation highlights certain important components of post-war economic growth, it is obviously unsatisfactory to attempt to understand post-war business in France on the basis of these factors alone. The argument of this chapter is that the modifications of the actions of the three main economic actors – businessmen, employees and the state – and the relations among them constitute an essential part of the overall development of post-war business in France.

'LE PATRONAT S'AFFIRME'

As has already been suggested, businessmen in France have never enjoyed a high social standing, but their status in the immediate post-war period was at its lowest possible ebb. Not only were they considered to be engaged in an intrinsically dubious activity, but the collaboration of many of them in the *comités d'organisation* under Vichy could only serve to underline the questionable morality of the business class in the public mind.

The *patronat* took refuge in exclusiveness and secrecy, which means that there has been relatively little information, until recently, either on organized business* or, in particular, on the activities of individual businessmen.† However, given the

---

*Fortunately, three books have appeared since 1974 on business organizations in France: Bernoux (1974), Brizay (1975) and Lefranc (1976). All three bewail the former secrecy of the business world and the consequent lack of information. Before 1974 Ehrmann's book *Organized Business in France* (1957) was the only treatment available, though his main concern was with organized business as a *pressure* group.

†This bifurcation between individual businessmen and their representative organizations might be expected in many contexts but is particularly marked in France where 'there are two *patronats*: the *Patronat* and the actual employers . . . who are not a community, since the heads of businesses are above all individualists' (*Le Monde*, 10 June 1978).

existence of '*les deux patronats*', an attempt must be made to evaluate not only the changing image put forward by business organizations, but also the extent to which this image is reflected at the level of the firm.

Organized business in France is fragmented to an unusual degree, reflecting, first of all, local and regional divisions,* the important division between large enterprises and small and medium-sized firms and the bifurcation between established business and a young ginger group which, at various crucial periods, has played an important role in significant transformations of the organized business world. However, undoubtedly the most important representative of organized business is the present *Conseil National du Patronat Français* (CNPF) which dates from 1946, and which groups *not* individual firms, but rather the so-called professional and interprofessional business organizations at the regional and national levels into one vast federation of business organizations in France. It is estimated that the CNPF will soon associate the equivalent of 900,000 firms with six million employees (Lefranc, 1976, p. 132).

This reorganization of the *patronat* in France in 1946 was based on a declaration of principles† which is worth citing in detail, since it expresses clearly the business attitude of the time. First of all, the new organization would represent *all* businessmen, including industry and commerce and both large and small firms. Secondly, the CNPF claimed the right to be consulted by the government, in contrast to the neglect of its views since the Liberation. Thirdly, the principles of post-war planning in France were accepted, but serious reservations were expressed about the extension of nationalization. Fourthly, and in a related vein, the *patronat* requested a more flexible economic policy from the state, which should recognize the responsibility borne by the CNPF in encouraging appropriate business action. Finally, the CNPF acknowledged the state

---

*Bunel and Sanglio (1976), p. 83. There are 487 business associations in the Rhône–Alpes region alone.

†Attributed to Pierre Ricard, who was to become first vice-president of the CNPF.

policy of employee representation through the *Comités d'entreprise* (to be discussed in the next section), though it simultaneously affirmed that the state should have confidence in the *'esprit d'entreprise'* (Lefranc, 1976, p. 131). This declaration of principles is interesting, for it expresses the will of the main post-war business organization to take responsibility for its membership and to oppose excessive state influence in its domain; if the tone appears slightly petulant, it reflects the threatened position of the group at the time and the distrust in which they knew themselves to be held, particularly by de Gaulle.

In line with these principles, the CNPF was organized on the basis of a general assembly, which gave 15 per cent of the seats to representatives of the commercial federations, interprofessional regional federations and small and medium-sized firms. The remaining 85 per cent of the seats were accorded to industrial federations. This heterogeneous structure was presided over by Georges Villiers, an industrialist from Lyon. He was the head of a medium-sized firm and had been deported to Dachau during the war; he could not be accused of representing the domination of either large firms or Paris, nor could he be accused of war-time collaboration. He was to preside over the CNPF for the next twenty years. It should be noted that the goals of the CNPF were limited to the co-ordination, representation of interests and efficiency of business; there was no responsibility for negotiation except at the express request of member federations.

A major concern over the period of the Fourth Republic, the maintenance of the unity of this rather heterogeneous organization, met its greatest challenge in the pan-European ideas of the 1950s. The small and medium-sized firms, grouped since 1944 in the *Conféderation Générale de Petites et Moyennes Entreprises* (CGPME) under the leadership of Léon Gingembre but represented within the CNPF, were, of course, particularly threatened by the prospect of virulent competition; from the time of the early discussions of the Coal and Steel Community they were resolutely opposed to the opening of frontiers.

Gingembre gave graphic expression to this opposition: 'The first wagon which crossed the border after the opening of the Common Market did not only carry European coal; it carried also the cadaver of French industry' (quoted in Lefranc, 1976, p. 155). In fact, while the CGPME continued to be represented within the CNPF until the revision of the statutes in 1969, it affirmed its right to direct dialogue with the government and the unions as early as 1948. The fragile myth that the CNPF represented all industry and commerce was exploded rather quickly, for this main business organization, initially hesitant about the European idea, came reluctantly to accept its advantages, influenced positively by the marked economic progress of the 1950s.

The CGPME was a relatively conservative representative of the interests of small and medium-sized firms during the 1950s; much more virulent was the *Union de Défense des Commerçants et Artisans* (UDCA), more commonly termed 'Poujadism' after its leader, Pierre Poujade. Through public meetings and the direct rejection of fiscal measures, the movement vociferously expressed the interests of small businessmen and craftsmen, which were threatened by the tendency towards economic concentration, and was particularly strong in rural areas and backward regions. The movement took on added importance in the mid-1950s, when it entered the political arena, first electing its slate of candidates to the Paris Chamber of Commerce in 1955 and then attaining a remarkable total of fifty-two seats in the 1956 National Assembly. In the late 1950s it declined to insignificance, but the force of its protest had its effect: 'As state intervention slowed down commercial concentration, Poujadism acted as a brake on the natural evolution of the economy' (Lefranc, 1976, p. 223). Poujadism was to return in another guise in the 1960s, but the movement rocked France by symbolizing the force of protest in favour of the small and weak against the giant institutions of society.

As to fringe organizations, the late 1950s witnessed a much greater consciousness of the role of businessmen in society and the emergence of the modern attitude of the CNPF. The role of a ginger group of young businessmen – the *Centre des Jeunes Patrons* (CJP)* – appears to have been important in encouraging the formulation of a philosophy which would legitimate the role of business. Thus we get the initial formulation in France of the conception of business as a dignified activity, at the service of the community; in this context, increasing production had to be encouraged, for 'in order to distribute wealth, one must first produce as much of it as possible' (Bourricaud, 1958, p. 906). Within the firm human relations techniques would have to replace the former authoritarian attitudes.† None of this philosophy was evident in the thinking of the CNPF of the time, and it may be easy to exaggerate, on the basis of rather scanty information, the intellectual leadership of CJP members. However, for the first time one sees a justification for economic expansion, notably lacking in the orientation of pre-war businessmen described by Landes and others.

If there were some aspects of the pre-war business attitude which had begun to be eroded during the 1950s, there was one sacred principle which was to resist erosion for a considerable period, and this was the idea of the unity of command. French businessmen have held strongly to the notion that it is their right and responsibility to take decisions unilaterally on behalf of their firms. This attitude explains, at least partially, the chequered history of relations with employees in French business. The period of the Fourth Republic witnessed the 1950 law facilitating collective bargaining, but the number of agreements reached was minimal and the resistance of the *patronat* to the negotiating pattern was acute. As Jobert (1973, p. 67) points out, 'Traditionally, employers tended to consider bargaining as an unjustified sharing of power.' And the union desire to negotiate some general issues at the national level was hampered by the limitations placed on the CNPF as a negotiating body. This stalemate between the *patronat* and the unions left considerable latitude for state action in this area, as will be seen in a later section.

*To become the *Centre des Jeunes Dirigeants d'Entreprise* (CJD) in 1968.
†See Bize (1960), and Bourricaud (1958 and 1961) for somewhat confused accounts of this change of mentality.

French business entered the era of the Fifth Republic considerably strengthened by the economic progress of the 1950s but still fragmented by the sometimes opposing concerns of large and small firms. It had modified, to some extent, its traditional attitudes but was still locked into unilateralism in decision-making; employee relations were to be shaken profoundly in 1968 and were to lead to the main change in the business class of the 1970s.

As has been indicated, it was really the period of the Fifth Republic that witnessed the most significant growth of French industry and commerce; some tapering off in the 1970s has reflected the general situation of the industrialized countries. As far as the business class was concerned, the period was characterized by the integration of a modernizing ideology from fringe organizations to the core business organizations. In particular, the CNPF was transformed from a beleaguered, defensive organization into an aggressive, initiating body and came to broadcast a management ideology of decentralization, concern for the employee and responsiveness to the environment. These tenets were well expressed at the 1977 meetings of the CNPF:

> President Ceyrac stressed the need for a thorough reform of the enterprise in order to meet more fully the aspirations of today's men who do not want their work to be merely a means of livelihood. M. Ceyrac also asked the heads of firms, owners and managers to assume greater social, cultural and even political responsibilities within the community (*Le Monde*, 17 October 1977).

The mechanisms for fulfilling the demands of such principles would be to accord greater initiative and responsibility to individual employees through the constitution of autonomous work units and employee participation in their planning, and to recognize that 'the enterprises need the understanding and the support of the French people'.

At least at the level of ideology, the French business class has reduced the gap between it and business groups of the other main industrialized countries. Certainly, the economic progress of the 1950s and 1960s coincided with the gradual strengthening of the *patronat*, and as the French came to take pride in comparative economic prosperity, public denigration of the role of business in society was attenuated, assisted by the legitimation for the role of business developed by the *patronat*.

However, spontaneous recovery is hardly an accurate image of post-war industrial development in France. As will be considered in detail in a later section, the state has poked, prodded and pestered French industrialists towards a modernizing stance. The state is dominant to a greater degree in France than in any other Western industrialized country, and the business sector has been a main focus of its attention. The *patronat* respond with a continuing stance of *recours à l'Etat*,* such that the initiative of the state versus that of business is often difficult to disentangle. But it is not only the state's official actions that have strongly influenced business ideology; its agents, in their para-official capacity, have frequently been in the vanguard of reflection about the business sector. One of the most influential books on business of the 1960s was *Pour une réforme de l'entreprise* by François Bloch-Laîné, an eminent serving civil servant of the time, which 'exploded' into the business world in 1963. It was specifically designed to stimulate reflection and experimentation and prefigured a great deal of later thinking about the restructuring of the firm. In some ways it was the precursor of the *Commission Sudreau*, appointed in 1974 by President Giscard d'Estaing, with a fairly open mandate to consider the reform of business in France. This commission, which reported in 1975, was clearly out of tune with the attitudes and inclinations of the *patronat*; its key recommendation (that of *co-surveillance*, to be effected by the presence of four employee representatives on the management board, as a means of control and of information) clearly went much further in abrogating the

---

*In a 1976 interview with an official of the CJD, ostensibly in the vanguard of business organizations, the response to a question about how recent ideas of the organization might be disseminated and implemented was that pressure would be put on the state to legislate the changes considered desirable.

sacrosanct unity of command than the majority of the *patronat* were willing to accept. The commission report has been buried beneath the weight of considerable public indifference, but the constant theme of greater emphasis on the individual employee (*'consacrer l'homme dans l'entreprise'*) has coincided more easily with the general mood of the *patronat* and has undoubtedly had an effect, despite the rejection of many specific recommendations. In fact, the *Commission Sudreau* may well have had more influence than is apparent at first glance by categorically going beyond the bounds of the acceptable and by encouraging businessmen in France at least to modernize in an incremental fashion.

The recent influence of the CJD appears to have been of the same kind. Its white paper, *L'autorité de l'entreprise*, published in 1974, also suggested a restructuring of French business, which was on occasion unrealistic, if not naïve, in that some of its recommendations were dangerous for the majority of the *patronat* (for example, the suggestion of the indirect election of the managing director of a firm). However, the debate occasioned by this publication was no doubt fed into the deliberations of the *Commission Sudreau* and, by proposing the preposterous, it simultaneously encouraged some willingness to change.

While one can suspect that the publications of individuals, organizations and commissions may have an impact which is difficult to quantify, there can be absolutely no doubt about the impact on French business of the events of May 1968. While the movement was originally directed at the state and the educational system in particular, its extension to the business sector is destined to remain in the collective memory of the *patronat* and has undoubtedly influenced the ideology of the 1970s. In a much more direct manner, it took the May movement to persuade the *patronat* to accede to the exercise of union rights within the firm – not only one of the most significant breakthroughs in the labour movement in France (see Chapter 6), but also the first acknowledgement by the *patronat* that their responsibility to exercise command did not imply a rejection of the unions' right to negotiate. While the concession was hardly granted willingly, it did indicate a crack in the enduring paternalism of the French *patronat*, as symbolized by the official rhetoric of the CNPF.

This raises the significant point of the extent to which CNPF rhetoric is translated into reality at the level of the firm. Is the French firm really operating *à l'américaine* in terms of structure and managerial attitudes? On this issue the evidence indicates a much less radical transformation than the business ideology would suggest; for example, an extremely influential report by two Harvard business school researchers (MacArthur and Scott, 1969) contains some withering criticisms of French business. While acknowledging some very real strengths, which include a particular aptitude for basic research, the confidence of businessmen that they are able to keep up with technological advances and, in particular, the very high level of education and the capacity for hard work on the part of leading businessmen, MacArthur and Scott delineate some basic weaknesses, which generally relate to an inability to adapt products to the market. Thus they point to the five main weaknesses of French firms as (1) the absence of management forecasting; (2) the minimal importance accorded to marketing and economic controls; (3) a fascination with innovative rather than marketable products; (4) the inadaptation of products to market needs; and (5) organizational structures which are far too centralized. In an analysis which is reminiscent of the American comments of the immediate post-war period, MacArthur and Scott link these weaknesses to an excessively rigid social structure (which is reflected, at the level of the firm, as a strict hierarchy), excessive paternalism and resistance to employee participation, the extreme inequality of salaries and working conditions, and a general lack of respect for efficiency. In effect, they suggest that French businessmen have only modified their practices at the margins in the post-war period (Mottez, 1961).

It might be suggested that a Harvard Business School perspective on French business is least likely to highlight any modernizing tendencies, and there is considerable resentment in

France of relatively uninformed critiques from abroad.* However, a more extensive study of French businessmen in the Rhône–Alpes region, undertaken by French researchers (Bunel and Sanglio, 1976) also provides evidence in support of some of the above-mentioned criticisms. For example, the authors indicate that about one-fifth of the 140 businesses with over fifty employees covered by the research had orders which would provide a maximum of one month's work for the firm (p. 380), a situation hardly conducive to rational planning and forecasting. There is also evidence of the continuing tradition of paternalism and of resistance to negotiation with employees. Of the top managers and owners interviewed, three-quarters claimed to be in favour of employee contracts, but fewer than one-third had actually signed such contracts in their firms (p. 445). Furthermore, despite legal directives to the contrary, a significant number of firms (11 per cent) had made absolutely no provision for employee representation. The authors comment on the businessmen's view of the firm as 'a neutral terrain, a human community which should remain outside conflicts such as collective bargaining' (p. 462) and conclude that, despite the rhetoric of the CNPF, the typical businessman of the region is not prepared to promote modified labour relations practices (p. 503). The conclusion is all the more significant since it reflects the post-1968 situation, cannot be dismissed as dated by those cataclysmic events and provides real evidence of the resistance to change of practices (as distinct from rhetoric).

Also mitigating the rhetorical image of change is another important theme which runs through the post-war period: the continuing bifurcation of interests between small and large business, with the *Syndicat Patronal des Petites et Moyennes*

---

*MacArthur and Scott interviewed about fifty French businessmen over a period of three years during the course of their research. However, the Planning Commission (*Commissariat Général du Plan*) thought their work sufficiently important to request a special report based on the research. One might add that France's own 1969 Montjoie report on industrial development is no more complimentary on the topic of French business (cf. Renaudin, 1969).

Industries (PMI) characterizing the CNPF ideology as a 'smokescreen' for the real problems of contemporary business in France. Even more telling evidence of the continuing force of the particular interests of the smaller firms was the rebirth of 'Poujadism' in a new guise in the late 1960s, this time led by Gérard Nicoud and his *Comité d'Information et de Défense* (CID), which fused with the *Union Nationale des Travailleurs Indépendants* (UNATI) in 1970. Though less spectacular in the political arena than the original 'Poujadism', the CID–UNATI made amazingly rapid progress, once again in the less developed regions, and Nicoud appears to have had sufficient ebullience to bring the interests of the smaller and medium-sized firms to the personal attention of political leaders. Certainly, the thrust towards modernization of business in France can never ignore the continuing reality of the presence and importance of small firms,* for which the CNPF ideology would be more or less irrelevant.

In all fairness, there is some scattered information about businessmen for whom the principles of human relations and of the later organizational psychologists are part of reality and not just rhetoric. For example, accounts of two extremely successful French firms (*Le Monde*, 21 February 1978), underline the deft use of human relations techniques, considerable attention to marketing strategies and a strong emphasis on consensus management (neither firm is unionized). This practice is obviously closer to CNPF ideology, but it is extraordinary enough to be singled out in the French context and for *Le Monde* to say of the directors: 'Miracle workers? Certainly not. But undoubtedly entrepreneurs.' And this is perhaps the most significant change of the Fifth Republic – that the aspiration to the classic entrepreneurial image is much more prevalent, much more widely disseminated and far more positively viewed in the

---

*The evidence suggests that there has been relatively little change in the overall structure of French business, despite some attempts at concentration in the post-war period, and many would argue that the percentage of small firms has hardly changed during the present century (cf. Savage, 1975, p. 145).

French context now than in any previous period. However, the restraining effects of traditional practices, particularly in the area of employee relations, are still strong.

EMPLOYEE REPRESENTATION*

The post-war pattern of employee representation is the combination of a state strategy aimed at containing worker militancy and a strong resistance to negotiation on the part of the *patronat*. The major developments of the containment strategy are linked to political radicalism and, in particular, to perceived increases in leftist political strength; they are *legislated* developments. These developments, in turn, have reacted upon, and been influenced by, the desperate resistance of the *patronat* to direct negotiation with the workers.

In some ways, French legislation has been characterized by *avant-garde* practices in employee representation which are astounding at first glance. In particular, long before employee participation became a fashionable managerial ideology, France had legislated provisions for two kinds of direct employee participation. Following the worker militancy of 1936, a provision for *délégués du personnel* (DP) was promulgated, with the specific intention that such delegates should represent the interests of workers and should provide a channel for demands if decisions were taken which ran counter to the interests of employees. In 1945, as part of the post-war reforms,† legislation required that all firms with over fifty employees should have a *comité d'entreprise* (CE), which was viewed as an instrument of co-operation between businessmen and workers that, as a consultative body, should give its opinion on the technical and

---

*This section deals in particular with various modes of employee representation at the level of the firm; for a general view of labour relations and the labour movement, see Chapter 6.

†Later transposed to the public sector as the *commissions administratives paritaires* (cf. Chapter 4).

economic situation, the organization and the working conditions of the firm. With a majority of employee representatives and presided over by the *patron*, the CEs were designed as a channel of information and opinion.

However, the legislative provisions are not very helpful in providing an accurate picture of the situation. As Adam and Lucas (1976) point out: 'France is probably one of the industrialized countries in which it is most difficult to deduce the real state of relationships within the firm from the mere knowledge of legal regulations' (p. 87). While accurate figures are difficult to obtain, it has been estimated that in the 1970s anything from a quarter (Petitguyot, 1976, p. 247) to a half (Adam and Lucas, 1976, p 81) of the appropriate firms do not have a CE. The lack of precision in statistics arises from the fact that the *inspection du travail* can only publish figures on the basis of the elections, on which information is forwarded to the Ministry – and this is a haphazard process. There is some indication that the CEs are more common in the larger firms and that about 80 per cent of workers are nevertheless covered, but this estimate is possibly even less precise. The absence of the appropriate CEs in a significant number of firms arises from the limits that have been imposed on sanctions; managerial person- nel are only subject to sanctions if they prevent or delay the appropriate elections and not if they fail to organize the relevant structures.

The *inspecteurs du travail* can be similarly passive and, in practice, only provide technical assistance once the employer has made the decision to organize an election. In these circumstances it is not at all surprising that the spirit of the law is not followed in practice. There is some indication that the 1966 reform of the CEs, by providing for more extensive economic information to be available to the committees, further strengthened the structure, but there is still a yawning gap between legislative provisions and reality.

However, more important is the curious way in which this consultation structure is intertwined with the union structure at the level of the firm. DPs and CEs are elected on the basis of union lists on the first ballot, non-union lists being eligible for a second ballot only if a quorum is not attained on the first – a rare occurrence, particularly in larger firms. But in this way negotiating and consultative structures are inextricably linked. The early development of the CEs was influenced by the *patronat*'s resentment of the CEs on any basis, accentuated by their spirit of confrontation rather than the consultation originally envisaged. The lack of rigour in the application of the law reflects this delicate situation and explains the practice of the *inspecteurs du travail* in not forcing the formation of the structure. But, at the very least, there is some ambiguity concerning the role of the CEs; in whose interests do they operate? And this ambiguity highlights their real significance: their existence has acted as a brake on the development of union structures at the level of the firm and has delayed the negotiation process between management and workers in individual firms. And their continuing existence, even after the 1968 recognition of the *Section Syndicale d'Entreprise* (SSE), provides a choice between negotiation and consultation structures, and the still traditional *patronat* obviously prefer the latter if they are forced to choose. This dialectical relationship between the CEs and the union structure at the firm level has attracted relatively little comment in France; Sellier (1976, p. 7) points out: 'The creation of delegates and committees, including direct representatives of the workforce, ... was clearly intended in 1936, and then in 1945, to compete with the trade unions.' But the amazing absence of official recognition of union locals in France until 1968 is surely due, very largely, to this containment strategy, with the consequent lack of detailed collective agreements.

The success of this containment policy is also illustrated by the kinds of issues that have preoccupied the CEs. According to Montuclard (1965), the main focus of interest has been technical and economic questions rather than questions pertaining to working conditions (including salary questions). In fact, Montuclard is extremely impressed by how extraordinarily well informed employee representatives on the committees that he studied were, and claims that they often made better evaluations of technical and market forces than management, also acting as active defenders of their firm or sector of activity during moments of crisis. (He appears not to have noticed that such extreme integration into the concerns of the firm as a whole simultaneously bears witness to the success of the containment strategy.)

In terms of relations between businessmen and workers, the post-war period has been characterized until recently by the extreme scarcity of forums for negotiation. Remembering that the CNPF, as originally constituted, had no generalized responsibility for negotiation on behalf of its adherents, little possibility for agreements at the national level existed. Simultaneously, the lack of union structures at the level of the firm militated against local agreements. Accordingly, the only real possibility was negotiation between a professional federation and union representatives at the level of a specific branch of activity, but such negotiation was regarded as relatively unsatisfactory by the unions, and very few agreements were signed.*

In effect, there was practically no dialogue between businessmen and employees. The real change has taken place in the post-1968 period; preferring some dialogue to violent protest, the 1969 reform of the CNPF gave this organization the right to negotiate and to commit its members on questions of social policy, though the issue of salaries was still excluded. Simultaneously, official recognition of union structures at the level of the firm in 1968, followed by the law of 1971 which provided for the possibility of contractual agreements at this level, have completely transformed negotiating structures in France. The *leitmotiv* of post-1968 labour relations in France has been the opportunity for both sides to engage in a dialogue. This does not mean that the *patronat* have been completely jolted out of their resistance to negotiation, or that they are generally providing workers with the protection afforded by

*Jobert (1973) records two such agreements before 1968.

collective agreements, but rather that the modernization of negotiating structures provides for an exchange between the two sides which was previously rare.

'RECOURS À L'ETAT'

As has been suggested, the business sector in France has been strongly marked by state action in the post-war period. Such action has combined direct influence through planning and other initiatives with indirect influence occasioned by political decisions. These decisions (particularly the decision to enter the EEC and to expose French business to completely new competition) have profoundly modified the whole context of the operation of the business sector. In general, in the business sphere the state has been an omnipresent actor, without whose intervention the transformation of the past thirty years could not have taken place. There is some indication that the traditionally *dirigiste* nature of state action has begun to be modified in the 1970s, but the tradition dies hard, and the recognition of the state as a far more significant actor in the business sphere in France than in any other Western industrialized nation must be acknowledged if we are to arrive at any clear understanding of French business.

Undoubtedly, the most significant expression of state action has been the planning process, initiated in 1946. Its main characteristic is '*la concertation*': collective discussion among the main socio-economic actors and the government on the salient problems of development in France. The planning process is effected through four main structures: (1) the *Commissariat Général du Plan* which, with a limited professional staff of about seventy-five, is responsible for the overall formulation of the successive series of plans; (2) the supporting ministries, particularly the Ministry of Economy and Finances and its associated bodies, which provide technical information; (3) the consultative structures, which now associate some 5000 representatives of unions, employers and various professional and other groups in a series of *commissions de modernisation* and their related study groups; and (4) the political structure, which (theoretically at least) takes the final decision about any plan to be adopted. Once again the expertise of the bureaucracy tends to dominate (cf. Chapter 4), and there is considerable concern that the process limits Parliament to controlling and implementing aspects of the plan rather than permitting it to influence content to any marked degree. The structures are interesting not only for the illustration of bureaucratic dominance that they provide, but also for their 'participatory' nature. In effect, the system of associating the main economic actors in the planning process has undoubtedly had a most significant psychological effect on those involved, quite apart from any direct influence on business that planning decisions may have exerted; it is a most effective way of integrating various types of experts into the process and of mitigating potential conflict. As Hamon (1966) points out: 'the leaders of the Fifth Republic wanted to reduce the bitterness of social conflict in France through an awareness of shared objectives and through a measure of co-operation – they have clearly used a means conducive to this end' (p. 224).

Now in the course of its seventh phase (1976–80), French planning has not been static, and significant modifications can be detected over the post-war period, in both objectives and methods. Initially very selective, and limited to a few priority areas for action, the process has been extended to encompass not only economic issues, but also problems of regional and social inequality. In fact, starting with the Sixth Plan, there has been a continuing and increasing emphasis on the 'quality of life' and a concern with a fairer distribution of the results of economic growth in both social and regional terms. In parallel with this growing emphasis on 'social planning' has come an increasing flexibility of methods of action. Initially rather authoritarian in tone, the plan has moved towards a series of voluntary 'gentlemen's agreements' between representatives of the private sector and the state; these are legally unenforceable, but each party involved is sufficiently powerful to institute reprisals if the understanding is violated by the other. Hayward (1972) indicates that by 1969

> 120 programme contracts had been signed, covering 85 per cent of French industry. These contracts ... grant the firms or industries concerned greater freedom to raise prices. In exchange, business accepts biannual, bilateral re-examination, between the Price Control Division of the Ministry of Finance and Planning Commissariat on the one hand and a trade association on the other, of the extent to which firms have conformed with the plan's investment, production and export targets. (p. 291)

It should be noted that these contracts have not invaded the service sector of the economy,* and also that the bargains struck depend on the French tradition of state intervention to control prices, a tradition which receives strong support from French public opinion.

In general, then, French planning has moved towards a flexible, stimulating process which is designed to *orient* business development in the desirable direction rather than to force the private sector into specific action. But this planning *à la française* has also entailed a major modification of relations between the state and the *patronat*. Rather than the previous relationship between what Hayward terms 'a dominant government and a subordinate manufacturing industry', the post-war period has witnessed the development of 'equal partners to a bargain' (p. 287); or, in other words, concomitant with the gradual strengthening of the *patronat* in France, the authoritarian state has entered into an (admittedly still unequal) partnership with its former hierarchical inferior.

Planning, of course, is by no means the only instance of direct state intervention in the business sector, and amongst the multiple organisms concerned with financial assistance to the private sector,† the *Institut de Développement Industriel* (IDI)

*The total commercial sector, including wholesalers, retail outlets and other commercial services employed 19 per cent of the total working population in 1968 (Vouette, 1975, p. 169).
†Described, for example, in Turot (1975).

has attracted a fair amount of attention since its creation in 1970. Sharing many characteristics with its British, Belgian and Italian counterparts, the IDI was set up with the purpose of accelerating the rate of growth of French industry. With capital of 333 million francs, of which 85 per cent is public money, the IDI is controlled by a board, two-thirds of whose members come from the private sector, and is intended to undertake financial risks which are not suitable for traditional financial sources. The official statement of the Council of Ministers also specifies that the IDI is intended to assist small and medium-sized firms 'without excluding the large enterprises', though there is at least the suspicion that the larger firms, whose representatives dominate its board, have received an excessive amount of attention from the IDI. But what is interesting in terms of method of operation is that the limited IDI funds obviously act as a magnet for additional funds from the private sector; the very fact that the IDI – through loans, share purchases or the evaluation of particular firms – is willing to support enterprises considered too risky by private financial sources provides a necessary boost of confidence and attracts the participation of these previously reluctant investors. So that, once again, the state is *de facto* acting in partnership with the private sector, though retaining the initiative to define priority areas (for example, the computer and electronics sector, mechanical equipment, agriculture and food) and allowing the IDI to select the firms which should benefit from an injection of capital in order to accelerate their rate of growth.

This new rapport between the state and the private sector is articulated in its industrial policy. In the early period of the Fifth Republic the plan was viewed, in the famous words of de Gaulle, as '*l'ardente obligation*' and the industrial policy was formulated as '*l'impératif industriel*'. Recently accused by the opposition of not having any industrial policy whatsoever, the government issued the official reply that the 1970s have witnessed a re-formulation of industrial policy towards the more flexible perspective of '*le redéploiement industriel*'. In effect, the pressure exerted by foreign competition in the early period of the Fifth

Republic necessitated the formation of giant firms able to compete in the newly defined market. But recent developments, including the new significance of raw materials on world markets for the recently industrialized countries as well as the desire for a calmer, more humane and more equal rate of growth in the already industrialized countries, require a less rigid industrial policy. According to de Combret, technical consultant to the President, the new industrial policy implies that state intervention must become the exception, competition must be restored in all sectors and that size of firms must cease to be the ultimate criterion for aid so that small and medium-sized firms can be accorded their due importance (*Le Monde*, 31 March 1978). Or, to put it more crassly than does de Combret, the great push is over and French business must stabilize. And in this stabilization process the state will be less prominent in the business sphere, and both the gradually strengthened *patronat* and individual businessmen must play their part. De Combret concludes by asserting that the intervention of the state must not be made into a taboo; the state must obviously continue to intervene when absolutely necessary. But at least the aim of retrenchment has been expressed.

A balance sheet of the modernization of French industry and commerce in the post-war period shows a curious mixture of marked economic progress, a desire for change in the field of employee relations and pockets of resistance to a major transformation of power relations among the main economic actors. In terms of economic advance, there can be no doubt that French business has demonstrated the capacity to confront its foreign competitors and to overcome the handicaps of its 'under-industrialized' pre-war situation, having made tremendous spurts of progress in the 1950s and 1960s. The main impetus has obviously been the opening of the frontiers, which, rather than exposing the 'dead body of French industry' as feared by Gingembre, has brought to maturity the potential of the French industrial fabric.

But this modernization in terms of production has not been

accompanied by a transformation of power relations among the state, employers and employees. The appropriate aspirations are certainly present. State policy, in keeping with the general post-1968 philosophy, aims at a less dominant role in the economic sector and a greater decentralization of decision-making. The employer ideology traces an image of a responsive *patronat*, conscious of responsibilities to employees and citizens alike. French unions, with the new facilitating framework of collective bargaining, could aspire to their usual function in a modern industrial state; that is, bargaining with employers on behalf of their members.

As has been seen, however, the aspirations expressed at an ideological level are slow in percolating through to the level of practice. Individual businessmen are still constrained by a traditional preference for centralized decision-making and contracts at the branch level (which have less impact on daily practice) and by a dependence on state action to bail them out of tough situations. The state is still accused of being omnipresent in the business domain and remains ready to legislate changes in working conditions if employer/employee negotiations are unsuccessful. The unions are stymied in their rightful function by the continuing hostility of the *patronat* and respond by taking little responsibility for enforcement of contracts.

One might well ask whether these constraints matter. After all, if French business has faced and overcome the EEC challenge, the fact that its labour relations practices have not changed at the same pace might be considered irrelevant. This is presumably the point of view espoused by those who 'take it for granted that France is already an advanced industrial society' (Hayward, 1972, p. 297). But it can also be argued that the increasingly voluntary agreements towards which state/business relations are moving are predicated on a stable labour relations scene. And it is in this sense that the archaic elements of state/*patronat*/union relations endanger continuing economic advance. If the state and *patronat* – their public protestations notwithstanding – insist on retaining their habitual right to the ultimate power in various arenas, then the 'new dialogue' is merely a façade for an underlying volatility.

BIBLIOGRAPHY

ADAM, G. and LUCAS, M. (1976) 'Les institutions de représentation du personnel en France: bilan et perspectives', *Droit social*, 3, 79–91.

BERNOUX, P. (1974) *Les nouveaux patrons: Le Centre des Jeunes Dirigeants d'Entreprise* (Paris: Editions Ouvrières).

BIZE, P. (1960) 'Nouvelles orientations intellectuelles des dirigeants des entreprises', *Sociologie du Travail*, 2 (2), 122–40.

BLOCH-LAÎNÉ, P. (1963) *Pour une réforme de l'entreprise* (Paris: Seuil).

BOULARD, J.-C. (1975) 'L'industrie', in J. P. Pagé *et al.*, (1975) *Profil économique de la France: structures et tendances*, Notes et Etudes documentaires, La Documentation Française (4241–8).

BOURRICAUD, F. (1958) 'Contribution à la sociologie du chef d'entreprise. Le "Jeune Patron" tel qu'il se voit et tel qu'il voudrait être', *Revue économique*, 6, 896–911.

BOURRICAUD, F. (1961) 'Malaise patronal', *Sociologie du Travail*, 3 (3), 221–35.

BRIZAY, B. (1975) *Le patronat* (Paris: Seuil).

BUNEL, J. and SANGLIO, J. (1976) *La société des patrons* (Paris: CORDES).

CARRÉ, J.-J., DUBOIS, P. and MALINVAUD, E. (1972) *La croissance française. Un essai d'analyse économique causale de l'après-guerre* (Paris: Seuil).

CENTRE DES JEUNES DIRIGEANTS D'ENTREPRISE (1974) *L'autorité de l'entreprise* (Paris: Hachette).

CHAMBERLIN, E. H. (ed.) (1954) *Monopoly and Competition and their Regulation* (London: Macmillan).

EHRMANN, H. W. (1957) *Organized Business in France* (Princeton, N.J.: Princeton University Press).

EUVRARD, F. (1975) 'La croissance économique', in Pagé *et al.*, (1975) *Profil économique de la France: structures et tendances*, Notes et Etudes documentaires, La Documentation Française (4241–8).

Expansion (1968) '58–68: L'économie sous de Gaulle', 2, 109–22.

HAMON, L. (1966) 'Le plan et sa signification politique', in J.-D. Reynaud (ed.), *Tendances et volontés de la société française* (Paris: Sédéis, Futuribles).

HAYWARD, J. E. S. (1972) 'State Intervention in France: The Changing Style of Government–Industry Relations', *Political Studies*, 20 (3), 287–98.

HINCKER, M. (1967) 'Lignes de force et de faiblesse de l'économie française d'après-guerre', *Economie et Politique*, 152, 21–34.

JOBERT, A. (1973) *Syndicats et patronat face à la politique contractuelle*, CREDOC No. 4201, Division prospective sociale.

KASPEREIT, G. (1970) 'Les perspectives de l'industrie française', *Revue administrative*, 23 (134), 186–95.

LANDES, D. S. (1951) 'French Business and the Businessman: A Social and Cultural Analysis', in E. M. Earle (ed.), *Modern France: Problems of the Third and Fourth Republics* (Princeton, N.J.: Princeton University Press).

LEFRANC, G. (1976) *Les organisations patronales en France du passé au présent* (Paris: Payot).

MacArthur, J. H. and Scott, B. (1969) *Industrial Planning in France* (Boston, Mass.: Harvard University Press).

McDowall, A. A. (1973) *L'industrie française* (London: McGraw-Hill).

Montuclard, M. (1965) 'Le comité d'entreprise: à propos d'une hypothèse concernant son effet sur l'évolution de l'entreprise', *Sociologie du Travail*, 7 (2), 175–89.

Mottez, B. (1961) 'Le patronat français vu par les Américains', *Sociologie du Travail*, 3 (3), 287–93.

Notes et Arguments (1973) 'Les exportations française', 34.

Pagé, J. P. *et al.* (1975) *Profil économique de la France: structures et tendances*, Notes et Etudes documentaires, La Documentation Française (4241–8).

Petitguyot, B. (1976) 'Le comité d'entreprise et les conditions de travail après la loi du 27 décembre 1973', *Droit social*, 6, 247–55.

Renaudin, H. (1969) 'Le dossier du CJD. La politique industrielle: la France prendra-t-elle le tournant?', *Dirigeant*, 24 (5), 26—9.

Savage, D. (1975) 'Les dirigeants et la croissance des entreprises françaises', *Sociologie du Travail*, 17 (2), 136–49.

Sellier, F. (1976) 'Tendances actuelles du syndicalisme français', *Gewerkschaftliche Monatschefte*, 9. (Draft text in French.)

Sheahan, J. (1969) *An Introduction to the French Economy* (Columbus, Ohio: Merrill).

Taylor, N. (1961) 'L'industriel canadien–français et son milieu', *Recherches sociographiques*, II (2), 123–50.

Turot, P. (1975) 'Comment l'Etat aide les entreprises privées', *Revue politique et parlementaire*, 77 (854), 31–45.

Vouette, R. (1975) 'Le commerce et les services commerciaux', in Pagé *et al.*, *op. cit.*

CHAPTER 6

The Trade Unions in a Divided Labour Movement

Martin Kolinsky

Since the Second World War the labour movement has undergone starkly contrasting experiences. Immediately after Liberation it exerted decisive influence on the new framework of political and social order, but the unity achieved in the Resistance was dissipated within a short time. By 1947 the labour movement was smouldering with irreconcilable political and ideological tensions. It was unable to recover from its paralysis for over two decades, despite the change of regime, the growing economic prosperity and the reduction of Cold War antagonisms. The division between a well-organized Communist Party and a declining Socialist Party reinforced the fragmented pattern of trade unionism. During the first ten years of the Fifth Republic the weakness of both wings of the movement meant that labour was treated as a puny special interest; its protests and demands were largely ignored, and the social dimensions of rapid economic change were consequently neglected. After the explosion of the May–June 1968 events, which blasted de Gaulle's authority, the importance of the trade unions was acknowledged in legislation on industrial relations and in tripartite discussions with the government and employers.

113

However, because of their emphasis on political solutions, the major unions conceived of their role primarily as the political mobilization of workers. The effect was to perpetuate the long-standing divisions of the labour movement, despite the fact that the *Union de la Gauche*, the left coalition, appeared likely to come to power in the March 1978 elections. The recasting and revival of the Socialist Party (PS) during the 1970s, and its electoral alliance with the Communist Party (PCF), raised surging expectations of a radical change of government. But in the months preceding the election the internal conflicts came to the forefront with increasing vehemence to damage the prospect of victory and to leave an aftermath of embittered disunity.

The deep ideological divisions among trade unions perpetuate intense competition and rivalry, which is an outstanding characteristic of the French pattern of industrial relations. The largest union confederation is the Communist-led *Confédération Générale du Travail* (CGT). Founded in 1895, it is by tradition *the* trade union, and it claims to have more Catholic and Socialist members than its rivals. Communists were left in undisputed control of the CGT following a split in 1947 in which the Socialist leadership of the *Force Ouvrière* (FO) group left to establish their own confederation, the CGT–FO (Criddle, 1977). Relations between the two unions remained tense and suspicious over the following three decades. There was also an important split in the ranks of the Catholic union, the *Confédération Française des Travailleurs Chrétiens* (CFTC), founded in 1919. A dynamic minority emerged after the Liberation and pressed for secularization of the union and independence from the influence of the Christian Democratic Party, the MRP. Both objects were achieved, the former in 1964 when a majority decided in favour of a transformation of the union in the *Confédération Française Démocratique du Travail* (CFDT). While the CFTC has continued to function with a greatly reduced membership, the CFDT has grown to become the second largest union and has formally committed itself to a Socialist orientation. Of importance also are two independent organizations: the leftist teachers' union, the *Fédération de l'Education Nationale* (FEN), which left the CGT at the same time as the FO and decided to remain unaffiliated because of its membership balance between Socialists and Communists; and the conservative white-collar union, *Confédération Générale des Cadres* (CGC), founded in 1944.

Plural unionism arising from political and religious differences exists elsewhere (in Italy, Belgium,. Holland) and contrasts with the more united trade union movements of Great Britain and West Germany (Kendall, 1975). An interesting difference between the latter is that whereas the TUC has a special relationship with the Labour Party, in West Germany the principle of trade union independence from political and religious affiliations was established after the Second World War. The principle exists in France as well, but in a very different context, which is influenced by the tradition of revolutionary syndicalism. The original concept of revolutionary syndicalism was that the union, rather than any political party, is both the means of revolutionary activity (through mass general strikes) and the basis of social reorganization after the revolution. This concept, which gives primacy to the union as the essential form of workers' revolutionary solidarity, was enshrined in the *Charte d'Amiens* of 1906. Although revolutionary syndicalism had declined by the First World War, and the organizing principles of Socialism and Marxism proved to be far more durable, much of its spirit and ethos remains influential. The CFDT is the most overtly committed bearer of the revolutionary syndicalist tradition of union independence – to the extent that some of its leaders are concerned by the tendency of militants to see it as a *'syndicat-parti'* (CFDT, 1971). The CGT also acknowledges the principle. However, in doing so the CGT stresses the right of its members to take part in the politics of their choice and to hold important party posts. Since the Liberation a majority of CGT leaders have been active in the Communist Party, and after the 1947 split it has been an overwhelming majority. Reacting sharply to this situation, the FO has remained a staunch advocate of union independence. Although its sympathies lay with the Socialist Party (SFIO) of the Fourth Republic, direct links were consistently eschewed. Relations with the reconstructed Socialist Party of the 1970s have been much more aloof and distrustful because of the coalition with the PCF. Similarly, on a trade union level, the FO rejected the CFDT's efforts to extend unity of action because of the latter's limited agreement with the CGT. The FO's anti-Communism, which originated in the Cold War period and has not deviated since from its hostility towards the CGT, has governed its relations within the labour movement and has left it in isolation. However, in the aftermath of the March 1978 elections this stance proved to be in its favour, and it attracted some support from those who were disaffected by the political infighting experienced during the break-up of the *Union de la Gauche.*

The FO has been the main advocate of free collective bargaining and has consistently pressed for reforms in the system of industrial relations. But it did not benefit appreciably, in terms of increasing significantly its influence among workers, from the growth of collective bargaining after the 1968 crisis. Nevertheless, in the highly charged atmosphere of industrial relations in which the two main confederations, the CGT and the CFDT, aim at a fundamental transformation of the economic, social and political order, and regard the collective bargaining process as merely a school for educating militants in the refinements of the class struggle, the FO contributes a certain amount of hard-headed stability (Anderson, 1977). Its willingness to sign negotiated agreements makes it easier for its rivals to do so; and should one or the other refuse, it is still possible for the government to extend the terms to all workers in the industry concerned. This is, of course, limited by the fact that the FO is weak in several important industrial sectors, including metallurgy, electrical equipment, chemicals, building and textiles.

French unions are small by comparison with those in most other industrial countries. The level of union membership is between 20 and 25 per cent of the labour force, compared with nearly 40 per cent in West Germany and nearly 50 per cent in Britain. Union membership is relatively stable and predictable in the latter countries, whereas in France it fluctuates. Membership in the CGT approached two million at the beginning of 1920 but fell by two-thirds after the defeat of the general strike and the split in trade union ranks in the winter of 1921–2 with the formation of the Communist-led *Confédération Générale du Travail Unitaire* (CGTU). Membership remained very low until the 1930s when, in response to the growing threats of Fascism, there was a strong current of popular support for unity and membership rose again. The reunification of the CGT occurred in 1935, with Communists in a minority of two to six on the executive committee. The Popular Front coalition of Socialists, Communists and Radicals won a major victory in the elections of May 1936. There followed gigantic waves of strikes throughout the country, involving nearly two million workers and lasting well into the autumn. The reunited CGT became an enormous force of five million and won significant gains (including the eight-hour day and paid holidays) in the Matignon Agreements presided over by the new government. But the movement was unable to consolidate and disintegrated almost as rapidly as it had arisen in the bitter aftermath of the fall of the Popular Front government in 1937: the erosion of purchasing power; the deterioration in working conditions (such as compulsory overtime at low rates of pay in armament plants); and the fierce factional fighting in the labour movement, which arose from the international situation (appeasement at Munich and, particularly, the Nazi–Soviet pact in August 1939 which led to the expulsion of Communists from the CGT). By the outbreak of war membership of the CGT had fallen to well under a million, and trade union activity had virtually ceased. After the fall of France the Vichy regime dissolved the trade union and employer organizations. The response of the former was to reaffirm the principles of French syndicalism in the famous *Manifeste des Douze*, signed by nine CGT and three CFTC leaders (for text, see Reynaud, 1975a, II, pp. 28–33). It was an act of defiance against both Vichy corporatism and the German occupation. When the resistance began to be organized as a partisan movement, after the attack on the Soviet Union in June

1941, underground contacts between Socialist and Communist trade unionists developed, and the CGT was reorganized in April 1943. The Socialists were in a majority of five to three on the executive, but at Liberation the Communists exercised greater influence within the CGT as they proved to be much more disciplined and dynamic. The labour movement rose to the height of its political importance, and membership of the CGT again stood over five million, while that of the CFTC increased to three-quarters of a million.

But the hardships and political frustrations of the early post-war years led to increasing disillusionment. With the development of Cold War antagonisms, factional fighting inside the CGT became intense. By the autumn of 1947 the breaking point was reached (Lefranc, 1969). The strength of the FO was concentrated at the top of the confederal hierarchy in the central office. It was supported by only nine of the forty national federations, and none of them was a major industrial union. When the split came, after the failure of the strikes of November and December, the Communists had a much stronger trade union base than their rivals. Moreover, the decision of the FEN, which had a large number of Socialist and Communist militants, to become autonomous deprived both confederations of funds, thousands of active militants and a stable basis of membership. By 1949 industrial production was above the highest pre-war levels, but working-class standards of living had not improved correspondingly. Social security payments had increased, but the overall level of wages had not significantly risen. The long years of apparent apathy and inactivity which characterized the trade union movement in the 1950s may be explained by the defeats and disillusionments of the post-Liberation period. The CGT lost about two million members, of whom only a minority joined any rival organization. The vast majority swelled the ranks of the resentfully indifferent. This demobilization and the intense ideological acrimony which accompanied it were among the factors which contributed to the decline of parliamentary democracy in the Fourth Republic.

Mass mobilization did not occur again until the crisis of May

1968. Although the strikes were on a larger scale than in 1936, the trade unions did not experience a commensurate rise in membership. The claimed membership of the CGT during the 1970s was fairly steady at 2.3 million, and its campaigns to reach the three-million mark were acknowledged to have failed. It remains the largest union by a wide margin, though the CFDT has made steady progress since it broke from the CFTC in 1964. The 1968 crisis gave it a membership boost and by 1977 it had passed the 800,000 mark, not counting retired members (an expedient adopted by the other confederations to inflate their numbers). The FO gained as well from the 1968 crisis but to a lesser degree, and its claim to have almost the same membership as the CFDT is an exaggeration. Unlike the CFDT, it does not publish the details of its budget to show the sums actually paid in monthly dues. In fact, the FO is rivalled for third rank by the FEN, which has a membership of over half a million. Although its recruitment is confined to the public education sector, the FEN has always played an important role in the union movement; it is a bulwark of organizational stability with strong Republican, democratic and humanitarian traditions. On a smaller scale is the CFTC, the Catholic union which refused to accept secularization in the 1964 split. The CFTC claim of almost a quarter of a million members is again probably an exaggeration, as is (to a lesser extent) the similar claim of the CGC, which recruits among private-sector middle and lower management. The membership *claims* of all the unions totalled five million in 1977, out of a labour force of nearly seventeen million.*

UNION RIVALRIES AND POLITICAL COMMITMENT

The representative character and influence of the unions in the private sector are indicated by the results of elections to the works councils (*comités d'entreprise*), particularly as the number

Le Monde Dossiers et Documents: 'Le syndicalisme en France', March 1977.

of councils has grown rapidly from under 4000 in 1967 to over 11,000 in 1975. There was a corresponding increase in voters from 600,000 to 1,670,000 during the period. Abstentions are high, increasing from over 25 per cent to 30 per cent in 1975, but they occur mainly in small firms with under 100 employees. Among manual workers and employees (the *premier collège*) the CGT is by far the most influential, leading in all sectors except banking and insurance. Up to 1973 it won over 50 per cent of the votes (declining sharply after the 1968 crisis but recovering in 1970). However, since 1973 it has gradually lost ground, declining to under 45 per cent in 1975, though it has retained its majority position among manual workers. The CFDT results were remarkably steady from 1968 to 1975: 19–20 per cent. The CFDT is second in most sectors, apart from banking and insurance where it comes first, and lies third to the FO in transport, rubber, food and agriculture, and public utilities. The FO and the CFTC have taken a constant share throughout the period: 7–8 per cent and 2–3 per cent respectively. The combined share of small unions, such as the *Confédération Française du Travail* (CFT) and the *Confédération Générale des Syndicats Indépendants* (CGSI), rose from 3.5 per cent in 1966 to 7 per cent in 1970 and then varied between 5 and 7 per cent. Sharp variations were recorded in the voting for non-union candidates, with figures ranging from 9 to 18 per cent.

The results for both colleges together (the second college includes foremen, technicians and *cadres*) show a similar picture for the period 1966 to 1975. The CGT remained in the lead, but declined steadily from 51 per cent in 1966 to 43 per cent in 1975. In both 1969 and 1973 it recorded lows of 41 per cent. The CFDT, FO and CFTC maintained constant shares of the voting, as did the CGC in the second college (taking 22–26 per cent during the period). Voting for non-union candidates fluctuated between 12 and 20 per cent. As may be expected, non-union candidates were more numerous in the smaller firms, particularly those employing under 100 persons, whereas union candidates predominated in the larger firms and consequently won most of the seats (*Le Monde*, 30 May 1978; Capdevielle and Mouriaux, 1976, p. 85).

The most highly organized union is undoubtedly the CGT, with powerful bases in the Paris region and close relations with the Communist Party. The vast majority of executive members of the departmental unions and federations making up the CGT are members of the PCF, which provides an important source of moral, social and political support. By contrast, the CFDT lacks both a foothold in the core Paris region and the consistent backing of a large working-class party. It has proven very difficult for the CFDT to establish itself in factories situated in Communist municipalities in the Paris suburbs. Although the CFDT has been able to recruit beyond the traditional Catholic regions where the CFTC was established, it still bears the mark of its heritage. The CFDT is strong in the Catholic zones of the east (particularly Alsace) and of the west (Brittany, Lower Normandy, Pays de la Loire), and is weak in the south as well as in the Paris region.

After the 1947 split the dominance of Communist militants in the CGT leadership was not a source of overt friction, despite the diversity of political affiliations (and non-affiliation) in the confederation. But dissent emerged during the campaign for the March 1978 elections, when Communists began to criticize severely their coalition partners in the *Union de la Gauche*. Socialists and others within the CGT were particularly infuriated when the general secretary, Georges Séguy, echoed the attacks and appealed to CGT members to vote for the PCF. A letter of protest signed by nine Socialist militants was published in the largest CGT paper, *La Vie Ouvrière*, in June 1978. The pressure was so great that for the first time opportunity was provided for prolonged criticisms both in the run-up to the Fortieth congress and during the proceedings at the end of November. Claude Germon, who had been a Socialist candidate in the elections and was completing a period of editing the bi-monthly CGT paper *Le Peuple*, asked congress what measures were to be taken to represent political diversity in the CGT more accurately, since 30 per cent of the members had voted for the PS at the March elections. He wanted the leadership to explain why all the general secretaries of the departmental unions and federations, without exception, belonged to the same party, and he insisted that the method of co-optation was no longer suitable (*Le Monde*, 29 November 1978). The point was received with hoots and whistles of disapproval, but it could not be ignored. In his closing speech Séguy struck a conciliatory note, recommending that congress approve the better representation of the various currents of thought on the executive committee (*'il n'y a pas à la CGT de privilèges se rattachant à une étiquette politique'*). He also promised a greater degree of democracy in the preparation of future congresses and gave assurance that free discussion in the confederation would be maintained. This seemed to satisfy most of the Socialists present, although there was unhappiness over the continued '*double appartenance*' of Séguy and other CGT leaders with executive functions in the PCF.

Internal dissent is clearly connected with the renaissance of the PS and disappointment over the failure of the *Union de la Gauche* at the elections. Whether it grows or is contained depends on the general political climate. It is clear that most militants are not content to limit their demands to short-term economic gains while accepting the leadership of reformist political parties. Their aim is to relate union activity to a struggle for the transformation of society. Membership of a union is often seen, in itself, as a political act – not necessarily as a form of party activism, but as a way of engaging in a struggle. Maire and Julliard (1975, p. 37) have emphasized this point:

> membership of a union does not bring material advantages and even has risks, at least in the private sector. To join a union does not mean entering an organization which offers guarantees, protection and defence, but means rather to participate in a struggle, and to become personally engaged in collective action. . . .

Although the degree of unionization is low, unions are influential and representative to a considerable degree, as may be seen in the results of elections to the *comités d'entreprise* and in the following of non-members when protests and strikes are organized. Militants are key figures, linking the union leadership with unorganized workers by their awareness of the latter's reactions and by their ability to 'read' a developing situation skilfully. The problem is that neither the militants nor anyone else know how many workers can be mobilized at any given time, nor if their following may be attracted by a rival union slogan or position. A union has no certain knowledge of its relative strength in any given conflict – it may be a powerful force or pitifully weak. The determining factor is not so much the extent to which followers may retain loyalty to 'their' union (most frequently the CGT), but rather the way workers perceive a set of economic/political issues. If the union leaders have not judged the situation correctly, the response may be very different from what was expected. A classic example occurred at the nationalized Renault plant in the spring of 1947, when workers followed the lead of an unofficial committee, forcing the CGT to abandon the government's policy of wage restraint. Since Communists participated in that government, the position of their ministers was made untenable. Again, in different circumstances, the unprecedented scale of strike activity in 1968 caught all the unions by surprise.

The problem of worker–union relations exists in other countries as well, notably in the context of unofficial strikes, when action is taken without union approval and sometimes against the advice or wishes of officials. The difference is that in the situation prevailing in France unions rarely attempt to impose such discipline because it is considered the right of the local branches to decide what to do (Shorter and Tilly, 1974). Moreover, given the intense inter-union rivalries, there is a premium on taking over incipient strike action as quickly as possible. Further, the general pattern of industrial relations and the very limited contractual obligations of a collective agreement (which do not necessarily require the signature of all unions to come into effect), place very much less emphasis on the notion of a restrained and temperate approach to the ultimate weapon of the workers. It should be added, however, that strikes are normally short,* partly because of very limited funds, and partly

---

*It may be noted, however, that some well-publicized strikes in which the CFDT was involved lasted several weeks (*Le Joint Français* engineering plant in Brittany in the spring of 1973) or several months (the Lip watch factory in Besançon during 1973–4).

because the intention is either a show of strength in a symbolic protest demonstration or an attempt to impose negotiations on company management, who are left much discretion by the loose guidelines of centralized collective agreements.

The French type of *syndicalisme minorité* has important consequences for every aspect of industrial relations. The low degree of unionization means that the organizations are financially poor, have relatively few full-time officials and outmoded methods of collecting dues and lack experts, research facilities and investment to supplement income. The CFDT is the only confederation to have a central strike fund, and it is small by comparison with British or German standards. The ratio of full-time officials to members is very low in most unions, so that the role of militants, the active minority of union members, is enhanced. They provide the essential link between the mass of workers and the union leaders, without placing much reliance on a formal network of field officers. As militants, they are by definition not negotiators seeking to minimize the political implications of industrial conflict. They are part of the grass roots, and have little or no contact with the more formal structures of decision-making and power. It is not surprising, therefore, that until the 1970s negotiations at factory level were rare. The situation changed to some extent after the legalization of trade union branches within the workshop and the 1971 law on collective bargaining, but the long-standing pattern of industrial relations remains intact.

TRADE UNIONS AND THE STATE

The intervention of the state in the relations between employers and workers goes back to the early phases of industrialization. Prefects and mayors, as well as deputies to the National Assembly, mediated strikes and attempted to resolve conflicts behind the scenes. If they were predisposed to sympathize with the employers, they were prompted nevertheless to take into account the workers' demands by a concern for the welfare and prosperity of their area. As one historian wrote, 'Whatever may be their own ideas or political inclinations, all try to bring the parties to a compromise, either by facilitating negotiations or – very often – by conducting them themselves. Not infrequently they are invited to engage in such action by the workers themselves' (Néré, quoted in Sellier, 1973, p. 90).*

With the development of centralized unions and the growth of industrial and social legislation in the inter-war period,† recourse to local authorities became less frequent. After 1944 the state's role became increasingly significant, with nationalizations, huge investment programmes and the development of economic planning. The private sector was enmeshed in the manifold influences of the state – financial, industrial, agricultural and transport policies and vast budgetary expenditures. Of immediate impact on the private sector has been the determination of minimum wages, price controls and price policies in the public sector, and the range of legislation concerned with unemployment benefits, vocational training, collective bargaining and so on. As indicated in the previous chapter, the state has become responsible for the framework of industrial relations. Although rarely intervening directly in negotiations (except in crises), the government encourages industry-wide bargaining and multi-industry national agreements (Dubois *et al.*, 1978, I, pp. 77–8). Moreover, it has the power to extend the result of collective agreements to non-represented workers in the industry concerned (even if they belong to unions which have refused to participate in the negotiations).

There is a notable contrast between the public and private sectors regarding the recognition of trade unions and the willingness to negotiate. In the former unions have played an

---

*See also Montreuil (1947, pp. 154–7ff.) regarding the failure of attempts to bring unions under the influence of municipalities through the establishment of *bourses du travail.*

†The main legislation was the eight-hour day, 1919; social insurance, 1928; unemployment insurance, 1931; family allowances, 1932; and the Matignon Agreements, 1936, which provided paid holidays, the forty-hour week, election of staff representatives and collective bargaining.

important role in mixed committees, and the rate of unionization is high (about 40 per cent). In the private sector employers have traditionally been much more reluctant to bargain and to recognize trade unions at workshop level. As discussed in the previous chapter, their attitude was initially characterized by a benign paternalism, which regarded worker demands as an affront to the authority and status conferred by property ownership. Therefore strikes often arose as a consequence of workers' efforts to bargain, and settlement tended to involve the intervention of public authorities. As a result, it was extremely difficult for unions to become established inside firms, and the development of collective bargaining was impeded. In the 1960s the unions campaigned for recognition of *sections syndicales* in firms, which the *patronat* strongly resisted. But, following the events of 1968, an agreement was reached and a law was passed to authorize the establishment of union branches in firms of fifty or more employees. Moreover, the law of 1971 enables collective agreements to be concluded at the level of a firm or establishment, so that there is now a legal framework governing workshop bargaining. But the preference of both the *patronat* and the unions is to negotiate at a higher level (industry-wide and inter-industry), leaving the details to plant bargaining, and the close involvement of the state in economic and industrial affairs generally tends both to reduce the importance of direct relations between employers and workers and to enhance the broader political dimension.

The relations between trade unions and government were profoundly affected by the establishment of the Fifth Republic. President de Gaulle and Prime Minister Michel Debré led the attacks on the Fourth Republic parties and sectional interests, which were deemed to have corroded national unity and impaired the dignity of the state. The new regime was determined to assert its authority and, in this, obviously had no sense of obligation to the established trade union confederations. Moreover, the political parties in contact with the trade union movement (PCF, SFIO, MRP) were in eclipse and had lost their influence. In the November 1958 elections the Communists won only ten seats and the Socialists forty-four. In the elections four years later there was some recovery, but it did not change the fundamental situation.* Further, the role of parliament had been sharply reduced under the new constitution, so that by contrast with the situation which had prevailed during most of the Fourth Republic, there was little opportunity for the opposition to influence the executive (even negatively, by vetoing legislation regarded as undesirable).

The role of the *Conseil Economique et Social* was strengthened in the new constitution. 70 per cent of its membership comprises representatives of interest groups and the remainder are government nominees. Trade union representatives constitute a quarter of the membership. But the *Conseil* is a purely consultative body, which offers its opinions but does not have a directly political role. Although it is noted for the quality of its studies, its advice does not determine government decisions, nor is it binding on the interest groups represented on it. The 1969 referendum proposal to replace the Senate by an assembly similar to the Committee was rejected, and all the union confederations were opposed to the idea. They saw it not as a means of access to economic decisions and political influence, but as a trap leading to a loss of autonomy.

Similarly, the role of unions on planning committees is advisory, and in general they do not attribute much importance to it. The CGT considers that planning does not make much sense under capitalism, except as an instrument in the service of the 'monopolies'. It has participated without commitment in order to gather information and to present its point of view. The FO, although attached to the idea of planning, has remained wary of government pressures which could interfere with freedom of collective bargaining. Whereas the CFDT participated actively during the 1960s, it has become increasingly disenchanted. In its view, the goal of 'democratic planning' cannot be achieved through collaboration or involvement in the

*In the 1962 elections the Communists won forty-one seats and the Socialists sixty-five, bringing the total representation of the opposition left (including the Radicals) to 147 out of 482 deputies.

mechanisms of '*concertation*' within the capitalist system. The attitude of the major unions, therefore, is highly critical of the planning system in operation and they are extremely reluctant to place confidence in it. In the 1970s the plan itself has become a symbol of the division between those concerned to promote economic growth as the top priority (the government and the CNPF) and those concerned with 'the quality of life'. The latter theme was stressed not only by ecologists, but also by the union movement, most notably the CFDT (see Reynaud, 1975a, I, pp. 268–72).

Although the decline of parliament and the strengthening of executive authority has provided greater scope for direct contacts between interest groups and the latter, there is no regular and assured contact. Much depends on the value which the government places on it, and since the trade unions have been seen as weak and politically suspect, they are generally treated in an aloof manner. The government has pursued its policies from above, as in the 1963 coalminers' strike, the 1967 social security reforms and, more generally, the question of wage restraint. There has been no equivalent of the situation in agriculture (which is discussed in the next chapter), where the government promoted the CNJA as a means of introducing a series of reforms.

THE 1968 WATERSHED

The first major strike in the Fifth Republic was that of the coalminers in April 1963. The government's requisition order was without effect, and widespread sympathy for the miners caused a sharp fall in the President's popularity. But this changed little in the overall situation. Labour was treated as a weak special interest, and was consequently frustrated and alienated rather than integrated into a prosperous, modernizing society. Despite rising standards of living, tensions were caused by low minimum wages, rising prices and persistent unemployment – and under-employment – among the young as the post-war baby boom came of age. Considerable dissatisfaction over conditions and prospects was experienced among various sections of the new generation (both students and young workers); employers' resistance to worker demands was stiff. By 1967 the industrial situation was smouldering, and there were some violent incidents. In a move which was widely felt to be arbitrary, the government decreed changes in social security which required higher payments by workers. The mood of confrontation was intensified by a recession in early 1968, which cause a rise in unemployment and further weakened the unions' bargaining position.*

The student revolt in May triggered an unprecedented wave of strikes, by comparison dwarfing those of 1936. Nearly eight million people, about half the labour force, were on strike at the height of the movement. After ten years of the Gaullist regime, state power appeared to be deflated like a punctured balloon, and a national jamboree of protest and strikes, anarchy, revolution and creativity was celebrated. Labour discontent and latent aspirations for industrial democracy fused in an explosive agitation which swept across the country. The government was badly shaken, especially when the Grenelle Agreement offering higher wages, a reduction in the length of the working week, a revision of collective bargaining procedures and the extension of union rights were rejected in factory mass meetings. It seemed to indicate that the strikes were not motivated by traditional claims, but the meaning was unclear. Only a few of the strike committees were organized in a potentially revolutionary manner – Sud-Aviation near Nantes, the Renault plant at Flins and Rhône-Poulenc at Vitry. The strikes were a groundswell which caught the trade union leaders by surprise. In contrast to the CFDT, the CGT disliked the spontaneous and anarchic aspects of the movement and strove to regain control of events by insisting on a return to work as soon as satisfaction was obtained on the basis of negotiations within the Grenelle framework. It warned against the dangers of ruthless repression and a military dictatorship and set out firmly to oppose

*For an interesting comparative analysis, see Soskice (1978).

'*aventuriers gauchistes*' who were deserting the interests of the working class. In step with the PCF, the CGT did not wish for the overthrow of the regime (there was a large measure of agreement with Gaullist foreign policy) and fought a war of attrition against the Trotskyist, Maoist and anarchist elements.

The CFDT, on the other hand, responded in a much more sympathetic way, welcoming the contribution of 'new forces in the struggle' which forced the government and employers to negotiate. CFDT leaders stressed that in order to guarantee appreciable results, a fundamental political change was required. They sought '*un socialisme dans la liberté*' and supported Mendès-France, who had been much admired in the 1950s when they were campaigning to transform the CFTC. The open response of the CFDT led to an influx of new members, which in turn created a certain amount of political tension within the union. At both the 1973 and the 1976 congress the union executive criticized extremists ('the children of Trotsky') for attitudes which threatened to undermine the role and purpose of trade union organization. There was a marked politicization of the CFDT during the 1970s, judging from the affiliations of the delegates to the 1976 congress. Of the 1900 delegates, 41 per cent belonged to a party, compared with 27 per cent in 1973. There was a considerable strengthening of links with the PS, a slight decline in membership of the more left-wing PSU and gains for the extreme left ('*les courants gauchistes*'). Two-thirds of the new adherents belonged to the extreme left, undoubtedly a source of concern to the leadership.

The 1968 crisis was resolved on two levels. The President exercised his constitutional right to dissolve the National Assembly and call new elections. The theme of anti-Communism was used effectively to express the threat to social order, and the parties of the left suffered a crushing defeat. Communist representation dropped from seventy-three to thirty-four seats and the number of Socialists from ninety-three to forty-four. The left as a whole, including Radicals, had only ninety-one out of 483 seats. On the industrial level, however, workers made signficant gains. The minimum wage was raised by a third, and wage settlements were of the order of 10 per cent. Although the Grenelle Agreement was not signed by the unions, it served as the basis of the industry-wide contracts which followed. Moreover, it clearly inspired the legislation of subsequent years: the December 1968 law on *sections syndicales d'entreprise*, the May 1969 law generalizing four-week paid holidays, the January 1970 law on minimum wages, the July 1971 law on collective agreements. There were also a number of national agreements, including one on job security (providing for joint employment committees and guarantees in case of dismissal or transfer), one on vocational training and a multi-industry agreement to improve the terms of manual employment by payment on a monthly basis.

Thus the government's attitude to labour shifted perceptibly, especially after the election of Pompidou as President in June 1969 and his appointment of Chaban-Delmas as Prime Minister. With the aid of his social advisor, Jacques Delors, the Prime Minister sought to transform industrial relations. The attempt to strengthen collective bargaining was notable,* and it included encouragement of *contrats de progrès pluri-annuels* in the public sector. The Prime Minister spoke of the full recognition *'du fait syndical'* as fundamental, promising that the government would insist on the application of the new legislation and would facilitate the regulation of conflicts and the functioning of the *comités d'entreprise*.

The mass mobilization of the 1968 crisis created a striking contrast between the ineffectiveness of the parties of the left and the enhanced importance of the unions. The contrast gave rise to strong pressures for a regrouping of forces. One manifestation was agreement for joint action between the CGT and CFDT. The agreement which had been reached in January 1966 (after the transformation of the old CFTC) was disrupted by the 1968 events, but re-established at the end of 1970 and given a broader basis in the summer of 1974. The working alliance with the CGT was set in motion after the 1970 congress, at which the

---

*For details of the collective bargaining process in metalworking, textiles and the railways, see Carew (1976), pp. 158–61.

CFDT declared itself Socialist and emphasized that its analysis was based on the clear recognition of class struggle. An integral part of the agreement was that open public debate could take place on the points of divergence between the two confederations. On a wider front, the 1968 crisis provided the stimulus for regrouping and unifying the political stance of the left. The absence of a credible political alternative was deeply felt and resulted in a coalition for the 1973 and 1978 elections and the 1974 presidential election. The basis of the coalition was a Common Programme, signed in June 1972.

SURGING EXPECTATIONS

The revitalization of the Socialist Party under Mitterrand's leadership and the second-ballot agreement with the Communists much improved the position of the left in the 1973 elections, bringing the total to 175 deputies (of which seventy-three were Communist and eighty-nine Socialist). In the presidential race of the following year Mitterrand lost by a fraction. These results made victory for the *Union de la Gauche* seem probable in the March 1978 elections. Before the September 1977 meeting of Socialist, Communist and Radical (MRG) leaders to revise the Common Programme for the electoral campaign, there was far more agreement than disagreement on basic issues (*Le Monde*, 13 September 1977; Wright, 1978). But the summit ended in deadlock, and disputes accumulated as the elections approached. Torn by infighting, the left was defeated, though gains were made. The total number of seats won was 201, of which eighty-six were Communist (Wright, 1978).

Although the push for coalition was strong throughout the period, trade union attitudes were not uniform. The FO refused to endorse the Common Programme of 1972 and remained suspicious of the PS *rapprochement* with the PCF and the CGT. It was isolated from the main political currents of the 1970s prior to the March 1978 elections, despite the fact that many of its leaders were members of the PS. Another factor in the situation was that the FO lacked an extensive industrial base, so that the PS found the CFDT potentially more rewarding in its search for alliances. The CFDT was more ambivalent in its attitude than the FO. Having formally declared itself committed to Socialism at its 1970 congress (the formula '*une autonomie engagée*' marked its resistance to subordination in a party framework), its leaders advocated support for the left coalition but refused to be bound by the Common Programme. The CFDT position was defined at the 1973 congress:

> The CFDT's view is that respect for the separation of tasks between the parties and the unions does not mean that the unions merely provide the workers' base, nor that the parties have all the responsibility for thinking about Socialism; in this domain, as in many other respects, unionism has the vocation of discussing on equal terms with the political parties.

The CFDT was adamantly against tying itself for a definite period of time to a programme of government, because that would directly threaten union independence by subordinating it to the strategy and objectives of parties. In addition, the CFDT was dissatisfied with the attitude of the left coalition towards *autogestion* (self-management), which was the cornerstone of the CFDT's political philosophy. The CGT and the PCF were scornful of it, and Mitterrand was reserved. Although both Communists and Socialists eventually came round to endorsing the notion, in CFDT eyes it seemed to be more a tactical manoeuvre than the acknowledgement of a genuine article of faith.

For its part, the CGT was strongly in favour of the Common Programme, and saw in it a means of realizing its own principal demands. But when the parties failed to agree on a revision of the programme in September 1977, and when CGT leaders participated in PCF attacks on the PS coalition partners during the election campaign, there was considerable unease within the CGT. The growing volume of criticism (mainly expressed by Socialists within the CGT) which preceded the Fortieth Congress at the end of November 1978 was countered by Séguy,

Krasucki and other leading spokesmen along the following lines: the Common Programme had *replaced* the CGT's own demands, a move which had eventually been recognized as a mistake; now the CGT could look forward to working for its own programme of demands. Although this explanation short-circuited the reality that the CGT Communist leaders were merely falling in with the approach of the PCF, it was true that the CGT had given the politics of the coalition precedence over its specific union activity. This is precisely what the CFDT had consistently avoided and warned against. However, such an admission was hardly forthcoming at the Fortieth Congress; instead Séguy announced a new effort for trade union joint action by calling for the creation of a new national committee. Since relations between the CGT and the CFDT had degenerated since September 1977 from an *'alliance conflictuelle'* to an *'affrontment ouvert'*, it was not surprising that Séguy's suggestion drew a very cautious response from Maire, who pointed to the continued validity of the 1974 pact. The CFDT leader then stressed the differences between the two unions regarding the analysis of the economic situation, the means of responding to it and the priorities of action. It was a rather bleak ending to a year which many had once thought would mark a significant political change, especially as the fear of unemployment had begun to increase the demobilization of the rank-and-file. In this perspective the projection of the aspiration for unity at the Fortieth Congress was an effort to consolidate a position in the face of relative decline, strong internal criticisms and widespread disappointment at the failure of the *Union de la Gauche*. Naturally, a smaller organization with a strong sense of dynamism and expansion such as the CFDT has more to gain from joint action and is keener on it, though evidently not at any price.

THE ISSUE OF MODERNIZATION

The economic context of trade union activity during the 1960s and early 1970s was characterized by high rates of growth, a vast expansion of trade within the Common Market and beyond, and rapid urbanization and occupational changes, notably in the tertiary sector. Not surprisingly, concern for modernization was shared by many different groups and penetrated the labour movement to some extent. In the words of one observer:

> Modernization has become a value in itself and provides a common ground for very different groups and interests: the CFDT wants to be the embodiment of 'modern' trade unionism, just as the 'young managers', organized in an association of their own, wave the adjective 'young' like a flag to demonstrate their opposition to old-fashioned employers and also their empathy with the 'young farmers'. (Reynaud, 1975b, p. 213.)

But this widespread aspiration did not by any means create consensus about political or social aims. It was simply endorsed as self-evidently a good thing – especially in its more limited form of enthusiasm for the benefits of economic growth – and, like planning, did not itself become an issue until the emergence of environmentalist concerns. It is true that there were always reservations on the left about the gospel of growth, as about planning, because of the feeling that these were concepts or devices used to maintain an unjust distribution of income and to perpetuate social inequalities. Such views were not pronounced until after the energy crisis of 1973–4, which gave prominence to the nuclear programme and brought in its train balance of payment difficulties, currency weakness and high inflation. The ensuing recession and growing unemployment intensified the opposition between those advocating growth because of the vulnerability of France's economy in international competition and those emphasizing the need to protect the 'quality of life'.

Some planners have pointed to a resolution of *la querelle de l'économie et de l'écologie*. For example, in Alsace, where there have been several demonstrations, René Uhrich has stressed that while economic development is indispensable to the creation of jobs and the reduction of social inequalities, it must be pursued with attention to environmental problems. His book

Pour une économie alsacienne réconciliée (1977) is prefaced and strongly endorsed by Pierre Pflimlin, mayor and president of the *communauté urbaine de Strasbourg*. More generally, the theme of 'quality of life' has been taken up by officialdom and resounds through speeches and documents like a new national anthem. The Sixth and Seventh Plans reflect the concern – without, however, specifying the means by which the 'reconciliation' of objectives may be achieved, as many critics have emphasized (see, for example, Green, 1978a, 1978b).

The tension has grown between the two goals because of the economic situation. The momentum of the ecology movement has highlighted some of the issues (nuclear energy, urban congestion, pollution and environmental protection), and it has added a further dimension to the problems of technological change and work organization, on which the CFDT has recently focused its attention (CFDT, 1977). More fundamental and widespread has been the discontent among the working population arising from the disturbing juxtaposition of affluence, unemployment and uncertainty. Although the outcome of the March 1978 elections deflated 'politics' by removing the prospect of a change in government, the initial placidity of the unions did not last long. The shocks of unemployment in the declining industries (textiles, steel, shipbuilding) were only partially cushioned by generous unemployment benefits, pressure on immigrant workers to leave and such measures as early retirement and temporary alternative employment. While the government succeeded in stabilizing the franc and balancing trade, it did not master those problems which had direct impact on labour: inflation and employment. The Barre austerity plan controlled wages and salaries from the autumn of 1976, with a certain amount of flexibility, through inflation indexing. Inflation, however, averaged nearly 10 per cent for the year ending December 1978 and had been 9 per cent the previous year; that is, more than three times higher than that of France's main trading partner, West Germany. During the same period unemployment rose over 1.3 million, the highest on record since the 1930s. Labour unrest over rationalization plans became particularly acute in the steel industry (Lorraine, the Lille area, Valenciennes, Denain) during the winter of 1979. The unions concurred in denouncing street violence and in strongly pressing the government to reconsider the proposed mass redundancies. The unresolved inter-union disagreements arising from the election campaign were overshadowed by the unwelcome policy of steel plant closures accompanied by hopeful promises of better long-term prospects (job-creating and retraining schemes for the hard-hit areas). On a wider front, numerous flashes of violence have been associated with labour unrest in various regions from late autumn 1978. The increase in social tensions may or may not have been directly caused by the government's determined pursuit of economic liberalism, but it is certain that the unions have not been always able to control the resentment and anger of many workers (*Le Monde*, 1 February 1979).

The changes in the pattern of industrial relations heralded by the 1968 crisis have proven to be limited. The '*nouvelle société*' of Chaban-Delmas, Prime Minister from 1969 to 1972, produced a considerable amount of industrial legislation based on employer–union agreements, but the persistence of traditional attitudes on both sides of industry limited its effectiveness and, in very many instances, seriously impeded implementation. The general failure of such legislation prompted President Georges Pompidou to replace Chaban-Delmas by Pierre Messmer, who proposed a much less ambitious programme. Within a short time political perspectives were greatly modified by the regrouping of the left, its gains in the 1973 elections, the death of Pompidou and the closely fought presidential election in May 1974. The victory of Giscard d'Estaing, under a liberal banner, coincided with the deepening recession. The perspectives for change within the labour movement as a whole were almost entirely concentrated on achieving political power in the elections of March 1978 (Lavau, 1978). The failure to do so has led to a search for a new strategy in the midst of disillusionment, apathy and frustration.

Thus the rooted conflicts of ideology and union rivalry have been perpetuated during a twenty-year period of significant economic and social change. The contradiction between the old patterns and the new context of urban concentration and industrial/tertiary development underlines the continuing *potential* for instability and crisis. The political changes which could give expression and institutional form to new social patterns and relations remain an elusive aspiration of the labour movement.

BIBLIOGRAPHY

ADAM, G. (1965) 'De la CFTC à la CFDT', *Revue française de Science politique* (February), 87–103.

ADAM, G. *et al.* (1972) *La négociation collective en France* (Paris: Editions Ouvrières).

ANDERSON, M. (1977) 'Trade Unions', in J. E. Flower (ed.), *France Today*, 3rd edn (London: Methuen).

CAPDEVIELLE, J. and MOURIAUX, R. (1976) *Les syndicats ouvriers en France*, 3rd edn (Paris: Colin).

CAREW, A. (1976) *Democracy and Government in European Trade Unions* (London: Allen & Unwin).

CFDT (1971) *La CFDT* (Paris: Seuil).

CFDT (1977) *Les dégats du progrès. Les travailleurs face au changement technique* (Paris: Seuil).

CRIDDLE, B. (1977) 'The French Parti Socialiste', in W. E. Paterson and A. H. Thomas (eds), *Social Democratic Parties in Western Europe* (London: Croom Helm).

CROUCH, C. and PIZZORNO, A. (eds) (1978) *The Resurgence of Class Conflict in Western Europe since 1968*, 2 vols (London: Macmillan).

DUBOIS, P., DURAND, C. and ERBÈS-SEGUIN, S. (1978) 'The Contradictions of French Trade Unionism', in Crouch and Pizzorno, *op. cit.*, Vol. I.

GREEN, D. (1978a) 'The Seventh Plan – the Demise of French Planning?', *West European Politics* (February), 60–76.

GREEN, D. (1978b) 'Individualism versus Collectivism: Economic Choices in France', *West European Politics* (October), 81–96.

KENDALL, W. (1975) *The Labour Movement in Europe* (London: Allen & Unwin).

LAVAU, G. (1978) 'The Changing Relations between Trade Unions and Political Parties in France', *Government and Opposition* (Autumn), 437–57.

LEFRANC, G. (1969) *Le mouvement syndical de la Libération aux événements de mai–juin 1968* (Paris: Payot).

MAIRE, E. and JULLIARD, J. (1975) *La CFDT d'aujourd'hui* (Paris: Seuil).

MONTREUIL, J. (1947) *Histoire du mouvement ouvrier en France* (Paris: Aubier).

REYNAUD, J.-D. (1975a) *Les syndicats en France*, 2 vols (Paris: Seuil).

REYNAUD, J.-D. (1975b) 'Trade Unions and Political Parties in France', *Industrial and Labor Relations Review* (January), 208–25.

SELLIER, F. (1976) 'Tendances actuelles du syndicalisme français', *Gewerkschaftliche Monatshefte*, 9. (Draft text in French.)

SELLIER, F. (1977) 'Principes et programmes des syndicats ouvriers français', *Gewerkschaftliche Monatschefte*, 9. (Draft text in French.)

SELLIER, F. (1973) 'The French Workers' Movement and Political Unionism', in A. Sturmthal and J. G. Scoville (eds), *The International Labor Movement in Transition* (Chicago: University of Illinois Press).

SHORTER, E. and TILLY, C. (1974) *Strikes in France 1830–1968* (Cambridge: Cambridge University Press).

SOSKICE, D. (1978) 'Strike Waves and Wage Explosions, 1968–70: An Economic Interpretation', in Crouch and Pizzorno, *op. cit.*, Vol. II.

UHRICH, R. (1977) *Pour une économie alsacienne réconciliée* (Colmar: Alsatia).

WRIGHT, V. (1978) 'The French General Election of March 1978: "La divine surprise" ', *West European Politics* (October).

CHAPTER 7

Agriculture: Problems of Modernization

Martin Kolinsky

The rural world has long been regarded as essential to the political and social stability of France. Agriculture is more than a special interest or merely one sector of the economy: it is a way of life, the basis of French civilization, the very cornerstone of polity and society. During the Third and Fourth Republics economic policy was framed to protect and to preserve traditional agriculture, and the Ministry of Agriculture paid endless subsidies and credits to powerful farm lobbies and to rural areas of electoral significance. The political importance of agriculture arose from the fact that until the Second World War rural France accounted for almost half the total population (see Table A below), and since then agriculture has continued to be over-represented by a favourable distribution of legislative seats. But in the Fifth Republic the long-standing network of relationships was severely disrupted by the policies and practices of the Gaullist leadership. The centre of decision-making shifted from parliament to the executive, and the old corridors of influence were blocked. Moreover, the policies adopted by the government were intended to promote *change*: to clear away protective devices in the cause of unbridled competition and to reform traditional farm structures. The assumption made by established farm organizations, that the interests of large, medium and small producers were welded together, became increasingly untenable as the government sought to promote a new farm elite which supported its policy orientations.

At the beginning of the Fifth Republic government agricultural policy was guided by strictly economic criteria, untroubled by electoral considerations. In the government's view, the problem was that whereas the degree of efficiency in agriculture was very low, it was imperative to give priority to farm exports within the context of the newly established Common Market. Many farms were at subsistence level, producing in traditional peasant fashion for family consumption and small local markets. Rural poverty, tiny holdings often consisting of scattered parcels of land, an ageing population and a low degree of technical knowledge characterized vast stretches of the countryside, particularly in the west, the south and the Massif Central (Klatzmann, 1972). Nevertheless, agriculture was one of France's key assets, and farm exports were crucial to the balance of trade. The establishment of the Common Market, by exposing French industry to the full blast of European competition, necessitated compensating mechanisms for agriculture. Georges Pompidou expressed it unambiguously when he was Prime Minister:

> The Treaty of Rome as originally conceived created only an industrial common market, which exposed French industry to direct outside competition, especially from powerful German industry. It was acceptable if compensated for by a common agricultural market providing our agriculture with important outlets at remunerative prices. The state is thereby relieved, for the most part, of the necessity to support our farming, and so is able to lighten the burdens weighing on industry. (Quoted in *Le Monde*, 29 July 1965)

In order to take advantage of the opportunities created by the Common Market, agriculture had to become efficient, competitive and modern, despite the social consequences of the fact that tens and hundreds of thousands of people would have to leave farming.

After the Second World War modernization of the northern regions was undertaken in accordance with the Monnet Plan. Cattle raising developed and sugar-beet production intensified. Amalgamation of the best lands increased the cereal crops. More wheat was grown under the stimulus of special financial inducements. But the less developed agricultural departments of the south, where a small peasantry predominated, were neglected and consequently stagnated.

The good wheat harvest of 1948 abruptly transformed a situation of scarcity, which had been created by the predatory German occupation and the immediate post-war dislocations, into over-production. Farm prices fell sharply and continued to decline in subsequent years, reaching their lowest level in 1951. The previous inflation had stimulated investment in machinery, and therefore the price stability achieved by the autumn of 1952 found farmers in debt and receiving low prices. Pressure on the government, led by the big grain and sugar-beet producers of the north, for subsidies, tax relief and price supports accumulated. Marc Latil's study of farm incomes (1956) emphasized that although small peasants managed to survive on such measures, the returns for them were very low (p. 297). Nevertheless, the peasants were predisposed to follow the lead of the specialized producers because the demands for price supports and surplus disposal were habitually couched in terms which invoked the misery of the small producer and proclaimed the preservation of the traditional family farm to be essential. These pressures interfered with plans for the rapid modernization of agriculture which the planning commission advocated, and government policy was increasingly entangled in the two objectives.

Towards the end of the Fourth Republic conservative domination of farm organizations – especially the FNSEA (*Fédération Nationale des Syndicats d'Exploitants Agricoles*) – was challenged by young, progressive Catholic farmers. Around 1956 members of the *Jeunesse Agricole*

Chrétienne (JAC)* made a serious effort to escape the confines of their organization and turned to the youth organization of FNSEA, the *Cercle National des Jeunes Agriculteurs* (CNJA). Their concern with land reform, the reorganization of markets and other changes brought them into conflict with the established FNSEA leadership. The JAC militants quickly transformed the CNJA into an active and almost entirely independent movement. By 1959 they had recruited the younger peasants, who had seemed increasingly apathetic towards syndicalism, in sufficient numbers to take control of hundreds of local organizations in the poorer areas. They were able to secure control of numerous departmental federations south of the Loire, thus becoming an important minority within the FNSEA. By 1964 their influence was no longer directly resisted by the FNSEA and a degree of power-sharing developed. Michel Debatisse, who was one regarded as a dangerous revolutionary, became successively assistant general secretary of FNSEA in 1964, general secretary in 1968 and president in 1972.

A comparison between the demonstrations in February 1960 and May–June 1961 serves to indicate the differences between the conservative majority and the CNJA. The first was the culmination of agitation in protest against the de Gaulle government's attitude to farm prices, which is discussed later in this chapter. The appeal for a tractor invasion of north-west provincial centres led to a serious clash at Amiens between riot police and 30,000 angry farmers. The demonstration was led by representatives of large farming interests, including leaders of the powerful sugar-beet lobby. More than a year later, the CNJA led demonstrations of small producers (potatoes, milk, wine, meat) in the west, centre and south. They were not demanding higher price supports and tax concessions because the question of prices was no longer taken to be the focus of

*The JAC was founded in 1929 by priests and established itself among small farmers in strongly Catholic regions during the 1930s. Although it initially supported Pétain's Vichy regime in 1940, the JAC later established ties with the Resistance. A vigorous, progressive leadership emerged, typified by René Colson (Colson, 1977) and, after his premature death in 1951, by Michel Debatisse and others; see Wright (1968, ch. 8).

concern. They were instead demonstrating in support of a constructive programme of land reform, credit facilities, market reorganization and the extension of social welfare provisions to agriculture. They also sought the support of urban workers, particularly in Brittany, where these demands were linked with a concern for regional development. Whereas the first demonstration underlined the depth of the differences between FNSEA leaders and the government, the second series of protests led to the appointment of Pisani as Minister of Agriculture and to the implementation of the 1960 agricultural orientation law. Further reforms followed; these were based on CNJA proposals and were known as the Pisani Charter.

The vigour of the CNJA and its approach strongly impressed the government as well as many writers and commentators. The government formed a close relationship with the CNJA, as will be discussed later. François Bloch-Laîné, a leading finance official, wrote in the preface of Debatisse's book, *La révolution silencieuse. Le combat des paysans* (1963): 'The young farmers are one of the main forces of renewal in our country . . . they are preparing an authentic revolution. . . .' The left-wing writer Serge Mallet and the American social scientist Gordon Wright saw in CNJA the possibility of a conscious adaptation of the peasantry to the conditions of a modern capitalist economy. The conservative leadership of the large farmers – who, in presenting themselves as defenders of the traditional peasant family farm, had been able to amass support for policies which perpetuated incoherent marketing structures and rural poverty – seemed about to be pushed aside. But others were not as optimistic. Henri Mendras, a rural sociologist, suggested more cautiously (1959) that the movement could be the vehicle of an emerging stratum of farmers on the British or North American model, because only a small proportion of the peasantry could survive the transition to modern farming. The trends of change in the agricultural population, as measured by the census studies of 1968 and 1975, lend considerable support to this view, as do the effects of modernization policies over the post-war period.

THE PATTERNS OF CHANGE

In the first half of the twentieth century the number of persons actively engaged in agriculture, fishing and forestry diminished from nearly nine million to five million. The exodus was a continuous process; as may be seen in the table below, France gradually developed into a society more urban than rural, though the latter sector remained important. After 1950 the rate of change began to accelerate as France entered a new era of dynamic economic expansion following its post-war recovery. A reduction of agricultural population at the rate of 2.8 per cent per year during the 1960s was anticipated, but the real change was much higher – close to 4 per cent. Between 1968 and 1975 the annual rate of reduction reached 5.7 per cent. The changing balance of urban, rural and agricultural populations (all persons living directly from agriculture) is shown in Table 1.

By 1975 farmers represented under 8 per cent of the total civilian working population, and farm workers represented under 2 per cent. The changes were by no means unique to France. Although occurring more belatedly than in most other industrial countries, the tendencies were broadly similar to those elsewhere (see Table 2).

The direction of change is also similar in advanced societies outside Europe. In the USA the farm sector decreased from 15 per cent of civilian employment in 1946 to 4 per cent in 1974. In Japan the decrease was from 51 per cent in 1947 to 13 per cent in 1974.

As the agricultural population declined, the number of farms diminished in France: from 2.3 million in 1955 to 1.55 million in 1970, then to an estimated 1.39 million in 1975. Although small farms still predominate (64 per cent of French farms covered less than 20 hectares in 1975), the *average size of farms* has increased substantially. The national average was 15.8 hectares in 1963 and 21.3 hectares in 1975. Regional variations in 1975 ranged from an average farm size of 53 hectares in the Paris Basin to under 15 hectares in Brittany, Rhône–Alpes, Languedoc–Roussillon and Alsace, and 10 hectares in

TABLE 1   *Urban, Rural and Agricultural Populations*

	Total population (millions)	Urban population (communes of 2000+) (%)	Rural population (%)	Agricultural population (%)	
1906	39.25	42	58	40	(15.85m)
1921	39.21	46	54	35	(13.80m)
1931	41.83	51	49	27	(11.50m)
1936	41.90	52	48	25	(10.58m)
1946	40.50	53	47	25	(10.24m)
1954	42.78	56	44	23	(9.65m)
1962	46.52	63	37	18	(8.36m)
1968	49.66	70	30	15	(7.25m)
1975	52.65	73	27	11	(5.89m)

Source: INSEE, *Les agriculteurs*, I (Paris: 1977), pp. 268–9.

TABLE 2   *Percentage of Working Population in Agriculture*

	1954	1964	1974
France	28	19	(1975) 9.5
Italy	43	26	16.6
West Germany	19	11.6	7.3
UK	5	3.8	2.8

Sources: OECD, *Manpower Statistics 1954–1964* (Paris: 1965), p. 24; OECD Economic Surveys, *France* (Paris: 1977), annex.

TABLE 3   *Employment in Agriculture by Socio-Economic Status and Sex*

	1954	1962	1968 ('000)	1975	1954–62	1962–8 annual rates (%)	1968–75
Farmers	3980	3050	2460	1650	−3.3	−3.5	−4.0
Farm operators	1920	1680	1400	1150	−1.7	−3.0	−2.8
Family helpers	2060	1370	1070	500	−5.0	−4.0	−10.2
of which:							
Men	697	406	298	125	−6.5	−5.0	−11.7
Women	1370	962	771	379	−4.3	−3.6	−9.6
Farmworkers	1150	826	584	375	−4.1	−5.6	−6.1
Total	5130	3870	3050	2030	−3.5	−3.9	−5.7

Sources: INSEE, *Les agriculteurs*, I (Paris: 1977), p. 21. Monique Gombert, 'De moins en moins d'agriculteurs', *Economie et statistique*, INSEE (Paris: 1978), pp. 19–34.

Provence–Côte d'Azur. The tendency to increase the size of farms is constant in all regions, though the rate is variable.

Taken together, the two trends of declining employment and increasing farm size indicate rapid gains in agricultural efficiency. The volume of production doubled from 1950 to 1970, while the active population was reduced by a half. The growth in productivity was a striking 6.5 per cent per year. But the social consequences of the rapid decrease in farming occupations have deeply affected the lives of great numbers of people. It is therefore worth examining the changes more closely.

As may be seen in Table 3, three million jobs disappeared in the period 1954–75. The annual rates of outflow have tended to increase in nearly all categories, most strikingly an ong family helpers in the most recent period. While some family helpers have become farm operators, there is no doubt that they and farm workers, as a category, are more prone to leave than farm operators.

The young leave, and although mobility is not exclusively the prerogative of youth, the ageing of the working population in farming is one of its most notable characteristics. In relation to the total labour force, in 1975 there were twice as many over 55 years of age (24 per cent as against 13 per cent), and half as many under 30 (16 per cent as compared with 34 per cent). The figures nevertheless represent a marked rejuvenation of the farm population during the period 1968–75: the average age of men engaged in agriculture was lowered from nearly 55 years to slightly over 45 years. This was greatly facilitated by government policy, which provided an annuity for early retirement, the *Indemnité Viagère de Départ* (IVD). More than half a million farmers received the annuity during the period 1963–75, releasing 9 million hectares (over a quarter of total farm land). About 60 per cent of it has been used for increasing the size of existing farms, the rest for new farming ventures. Originally granted only to those of 65 years, the age for receiving the IVD has been reduced to 60, or 55 in the case of widows and the physically handicapped. There has been a concentration of beneficiaries in Brittany, the Massif Central, the south-west and the Alps. In certain departments – Landes, Pyrénées–Atlantiques, Corrèze, Aveyron and Lot – about half the farm land has been affected. Young farmers between 17 and 30 years of age have been installed on some of the available land, at a rate of between 3000 and 7000 per year, which is very far below the objective of over 100,000 a year once considered desirable.

Male entry into agriculture continues to diminish rapidly: whereas the annual average in the 1960s was over 33,000, in the 1970s it was as low as 19,000; that is less than a third of those leaving through retirement and death. Female entry into agriculture is drying up: it fell from an annual average of over 13,000 in the 1960s to under 4,500 in the 1970s. The refusal of young women to remain in small farming has resulted in a steep rise of enforced bachelorhood. A survey in June 1953 showed that almost 60 per cent of married women whose parents were in farming had married within agriculture. But in 1969 only 21 of 100 farmers' daughters had married within agriculture. The rate of bachelorhood among farmers aged 40–49 years was 7 per cent during the inter-war period and rose to 18 per cent in 1968. However, the rate varies greatly according to the size of farm, and the probability of enforced bachelorhood is considerable only for the small farmer. The marriage rates of farmers working more than 20 hectares are comparable with the urban middle and upper strata. But for those on farms under 15 hectares the likelihood of remaining a bachelor is abnormally high: in the age group 40–49 years one out of eight farmers on 10–15 hectares is a bachelor, one in five on 5–10 hectares and one in three on less than 5 hectares where there is no specialized production (Jegouzo and Brangeon, 1978, p. 399).

In short, a small farm with low income makes heavy demands on the wife's labour, and she is often '*l'esclave de la vache*'. The massive flight of young women from farming is easily explained: poor housing, lack of amenities, shortage of money, long hours of work, few or no holidays. If the flight continues with as rapid a tempo as during the period 1968–75, the traditional peasant family farm, of such great historical and mythical importance in France, will become a rare species in another few decades.

The key to staying or leaving is the size of holding: the larger the farm, the less likely there is to be migration of farmers or of family helpers, and the rate of entry into agriculture of farmers' children increases with the size of the farm. Conversely, the youth born into the small peasantry are the most likely to be excluded from agriculture. Frequently they become unskilled workers; they are more likely to remain workers than are the children of workers in that socio-economic category. Nine-tenths of the women who left agriculture in 1959 were in unskilled or semi-skilled jobs in 1964, as were eight-tenths of farm labourers and six-tenths of male family helpers/farmers. Only 4 per cent of the latter and less than 2 per cent of the women were in clerical occupations or in the liberal professions (Jegouzo and Brangeon, 1978, pp. 384–5; Jegouzo, 1972, pp. 13–15, 23–4).

These occupational changes may occur without a deep sense of social discontinuity. A former family helper may continue to live with his or her parents while travelling elsewhere to work, or an ex-farmer may hold onto some land and become an '*ouvrier-paysan*'. Even if the occupational change involves moving from one's farm, in most cases it does not necessitate a change of department or of region. Geographical mobility is often limited to a change of commune or canton within a rural milieu. The reason is that employment (usually in building or public works, in food processing or transport) tends to be in local industries. A typical example is the car factory at Rennes in Brittany, which draws its labour from a rural hinterland as far away as 70 kilometres. The major inter-regional migration is towards the Paris region, but industrial decentralization in the 1960s and 1970s increasingly reduced the flow of migration in that direction. Agricultural exodus and rural exodus, then, are not equivalent terms everywhere, though they may be in some areas, particularly in mountainous zones (Jegouzo, 1972, pp. 28–34).

However, as will be discussed in the next chapter, the dominant trend is very rapid urbanization, and all but a few of the regions in which there are significant proportions of agricultural employment are increasingly more urban than rural.

Even in the most rural regions – Limousin, Poitou–Charentes and Brittany – the rate of growth of urban communes is striking.

MODERNIZATION POLICIES

The changes in the social structure of farming were the outcome of both the strong surge of industrial expansion and government policies designed to encourage the modernization of agriculture to enhance the competitive position of the French economy in the Common Market and in world trade. Industrial expansion had three important consequences for agriculture. First, the demand for labour in the building trades and industry attracted farm workers and small farmers, accelerating the agricultural exodus. Secondly, the decline in the farming population resulted in a growing concentration of land, which benefited the large and medium-sized farms. This was accompanied by an increasing use of industrial products in farming, so that the interchanges between the two sectors of the economy intensified. The result was an enormous growth in the need for credit. Farm debts rose from 11 thousand million francs to 120 thousand million during the period 1960–77, representing a rise from 5 per cent to 27 per cent in the proportion of interest in the total costs of production. Thirdly, the marketing of agricultural products was more highly organized, involving contract relations with food-processing industries. Whether private companies or co-operatives, these industries were concerned both with regularity of supply and with quality and were therefore interested in raising the technical knowledge of their suppliers. The concern to diffuse knowledge of agricultural techniques was strongly reinforced by government action because of the importance of farm exports to the balance of trade.

At the beginning of the Fifth Republic the backwardness of much of French agriculture was seen as an obstacle to economic expansion, which the creation of the Common Market had made imperative. The government's economic and monetary policies (inspired by the orthodox liberal economist Jacques Rueff) were to let competition reign supreme. Although industry faced up to such bracing measures as the removal of import restrictions and the devaluation of the franc, the reaction in agriculture was different. The slashing of market supports and the suppression of indexation (a sliding-scale method of relating agricultural prices to industrial prices, which farmers had fought hard to have established towards the end of the Fourth Republic) unleashed a powerful wave of opposition from the established farm leadership. The government's response was to limit the influence of the representatives of big farming interests, organized in the FNSEA and the cereal producers' associations, and to create a new elite. An alliance was forged with the leaders of the CNJA, the dynamic movement of the middle peasantry. As mentioned at the beginning of this chapter, the main challenge to the FNSEA came from its own youth group, the CNJA, which sought to adapt the peasantry to the exigencies of capitalist farming. Although the delays in implementing the agricultural orientation law of August 1960 was one of the causes of peasant agitation, mutual understanding was subsequently strengthened when Pisani, who served as Minister of Agriculture for over four years, from 1961–6, enacted supplementary legislation, drawing on ideas propounded by the CNJA.

The basis of the conflict between the conservative farm leadership and Gaullism was as much social and political as economic. The new regime, by concentrating power in the executive and by reducing the role of parliament, had threatened the status of the traditional notables in the countryside. 'They could no longer use the system of social relations to put pressure on the political class and to maintain the old equilibrium' (Gervais *et al.*, 1976, IV, p. 586; see also Berger, 1973, pp. 429–31). Moreover, in the struggle over Algeria many of the farm leaders were strongly sympathetic with the extremist view that Algeria should remain French, and they felt betrayed by de Gaulle's method of resolving the conflict. An even more fundamental estrangement from the government arose from the fact that most of these men had been involved in the running of the Peasant Corporation during the Vichy regime and, after the Liberation, had strongly and successfully resisted the plans for reform and modernization which the *Confédération Général de l'Agriculture* (CGA) advocated.* Not surprisingly, then, their opposition to the government's '*anti-paysan*' policy was embittered when the CNJA, which had a comparatively limited audience, was accorded representative status equal to that of the FNSEA, granted two seats on the Economic and Social Council and awarded financial credits to aid its organization and recruitment. All these favours were showered on the youth section of the parent organization, and its programme of reforms were finding a receptive audience in government circles!

Promotion of an agricultural counter-elite was not merely a political manoeuvre by the government because the CNJA orientation was shared in many respects by both. In contrast to the FNSEA, both agreed that for the majority of small farms high prices alone could not provide adequate incomes; that the economic future of France depended on a *transformation* of agriculture to facilitate the industrial development of the country. What was required was a new farm leadership, ready for changes, which would supplant the traditionalists defending their place in an outmoded *monde paysan* and still nostalgic for the Vichy Peasant Corporation. Politically, there was agreement on the need for the state to intervene to organize the changes and to cushion their social consequences, while at the same time permitting the individual to develop his own initiatives and

*The CGA was established in 1943 and published an underground paper *La résistance paysanne*. Led by Pierre Tanguy-Prigent, a Breton Socialist who became Minister of Agriculture, 1944–7, the CGA strongly opposed the Vichy Peasant Corporation. After Liberation the CGA became the central co-ordinating organism of farming interests. One of its constituent federations was the FNSEA, which became a focus of right-wing opposition to the Confederation's leftist leadership. The FNSEA gradually asserted its autonomy and established its domination in 1953, when the statutes were changed to eliminate the budget and staff of the CGA (see Wright, 1968, chs 6, 7).

responsibility. The alliance with the government was welcomed by the CNJA as a fulfilment of peasant aspirations. Two fundamental aspects of this situation may be noted. First, there was agreement that not all of the peasantry could continue in agriculture; only the most successful could do so – under the optimum conditions to be created by the government's programme. In other words, the middle peasantry was to be strengthened, the small peasantry eliminated. Secondly, the position of the middle peasantry nevertheless proved to be far more ambiguous than was apparent in the early 1960s. Since implementation of the farm modernization programme was blunted by the economic imperatives arising from the key role of the large farms in Common Market trade (an issue discussed below), the adaptation of the middle peasantry was more difficult than had been anticipated. A certain splitting of the ranks occurred. Although the main body continued to support the pragmatic compromises of Debatisse, sharing office with the big farmers' representatives in the FNSEA and maintaining the alliance with government, a number were disaffected. Some of the latter became apathetic, while others became more radical and either joined the Socialist Party or supported the Communist-led *Mouvement d'Organisation et de Défense des Exploitations Familiales* (MODEF), which was founded in 1959 as the co-ordinating organism of diverse peasant protest groups.

The organizational strength of big farming interests was reasserted by the mid-1960s. Frustrated by the decline of their influence in Paris, conservative leaders sought to obtain their goals on the European level, where questions of market organization, prices and methods of handling surplus production were being decided. Since farm prices were higher in the other countries, the agreed Common Market prices would necessarily be higher than domestic French prices, and this meant a very considerable rise in the incomes of those supplying the relevant products. Moreover, the Community represented a vast market, well protected in many respects from outside competition. The French big farmers did not realize these benefits in full during the early 1960s because the Gaullist government acted in Brussels as a brake on farm price rises. But by the beginning of 1965 the growing recognition of the importance of agricultural exports in the balance of trade and the government's need to reduce the opposition led to a significant change of policy. The French government agreed to a common European price for wheat to be effective from 1 July 1967, which provided very considerable financial advantages for the large farmers of the Paris Basin. In contrast, the liberalization of prices in the fruit and vegetable trade, to which the French government agreed, benefited the Italian and Dutch growers and was unpopular with the French peasants. Nevertheless, opposition to Gaullism among the big farmers continued and reached new heights, because the President precipitated a serious crisis in the Common Market by boycotting its institutions for seven months from June 1965. The crisis arose from the Commission's attempt to link financial regulations for a common agricultural policy with proposals for making Community institutions more independent and more effective. Although it desired the former, the French government did not accept the package. The French agricultural interest groups, however, made known their sympathies with the Commission and resented their own government's threat to the vision of '*l'Europe verte*'. They undertook a vigorous information campaign in the autumn of 1965, highlighted by the publication of a widely-circulated book, *Le Marché Commun et l'agriculture: Livre blanc des organisations professionnelles agricoles*. The message was unequivocal: the future of French agriculture depended on the Common Market (Muth, 1970, pp. 224–5). In the December 1965 presidential elections, which took place before the boycott ended, the national council of the FNSEA was hostile to de Gaulle. However, early in the new year the Common Market crisis was resolved on terms satisfactory to the French government, and relations with the agricultural interest groups improved. The reform-minded Minister of Agriculture, Pisani, was replaced in January 1966 by Edgar Faure who, as a prominent politician of the Fourth Republic, had close contact with the old agricultural elite. The common ground between the government and the big agricultural producers, which had been expressed with clarity by Georges Pompidou the previous July (*Le Monde*, 29 July 1965) was becoming more important than the plans for structural reform. Prices, after all, were given priority.

The agricultural legislation of the early 1960s* was concerned with major dimensions of farm modernization: land policy, social funds and health insurance, equipment and technical education. It was presented as a defence of the family farm, a time-honoured ritual, which in this case disguised the extent of change desired. Although a 'model' type of farm was indicated, care was taken not to define the level below which credits and aids would be withheld. It was not until 1968 that 15.4 hectares was specified as the minimum farm size for access to loans from the *Crédit Agricole* (Gervais *et al.*, 1976, IV, p. 620). What was accomplished was the rapid elimination of the least productive elements in farming, while the risks of widespread social conflict were minimized.

An important instrument of land policy which the legislation established, based on CNJA proposals, was the state-funded *Sociétés d'Aménagement Foncier et d'Etablissement Rural* (SAFER). These institutions are managed by professional organizations such as the chambers of agriculture, the co-operatives, *Crédit Agricole* and the FNSEA. They buy land at auctions, undertake improvements such as drainage and resell on favourable mortgage terms to young farmers or to existing small/medium farms. The effect is to limit increases in the price of land in some instances, to facilitate the process of *remembrement* in many communes and to prevent too great a concentration of landed property, especially among those whose essential interests are non-agricultural. By the end of 1975 the thirty SAFERs had bought a total of 828,000 hectares and resold 700,000 – the main activity being in the west and the

---

*Loi d'orientation agricole, August 1960; *loi complémentaire*, August 1962; and 1961 decree establishing *Fonds d'Orientation et de Régularisation des Marchés Agricoles* (FORMA).

Mediterranean Midi. On average between 6000 and 7000 farms benefit from the sales each year.

The SAFERs represented a new response to the problem of the extreme fragmentation of land, which has been an object of concern since the end of the First World War.* The policy of *remembrement*, or land amalgamation, was retained in the Fourth Republic by a law of 1951. Its original aim was to bring together as closely as possible the residence of the farmer and his parcels of land. The enlargement of farms, necessitated by the extensive use of agricultural machinery, soon became an important additional objective. The process of amalgamation was speeded up by the establishment of the SAFERs. By 1972 more than 8 million hectares were amalgamated, roughly a quarter of total farm land. The annual average for the decade 1962–72 was almost half a million hectares. Regional differences are marked. The process was much easier in the Paris Basin than in the mountain zones and the Midi, where less than 5 per cent of farm land is involved. By the end of 1976 the total approached 10 million hectares, about 30 per cent of French farm land, and operations under way amounted to another million hectares. The pattern of regional variation has not changed fundamentally, although the process has significantly accelerated in Brittany, affecting 40 per cent of its farmland.

In 1967 the *Centre National pour l'Aménagement des Structures des Exploitations Agricoles* took charge of the whole range of state aids for the modernization of farm holdings initiated by the 1960 law. The aids may be grouped into the following categories: the IVD, which (as mentioned above) encourages retirement by the payment of annuities; occupational training to help people leaving farms to prepare for non-agricultural employment; and aids for '*promotion*' which include help for young farmers with diplomas, the conversion of

---

*The law of November 1918 was effective in the war-devastated areas but not elsewhere because financial inducements were not offered and the consent of a majority of landowners in a locality was required (see Gervais *et al.*, 1976, IV, p. 543).

old farms, the re-establishment of farmers in more favourable farming areas and the launching of new products. There are also programmes of '*opérations groupées*', which bring together a package of aids to facilitate renewal at a communal level.

On a larger scale, the fund for rural renewal, with the co-operation of the *Délégation à l'Aménagement du Territoire et à l'Action Regionale* (DATAR),* launched integrated modernization schemes in major zones of rural poverty: Brittany, Corsica, the mountainous zones (those of the Massif Central, Vosges and Jura, north and south Alps and the Pyrenees), areas contiguous with mountain zones and those adjacent to the national parks. The objectives were multiple: to improve roads, communications and public services; to renovate villages and rural centres; to improve education and training in rural areas; to encourage the rationalization and modernization of agriculture; and to provide alternative employment by developing industry, crafts, tourism and the tertiary sector in rural areas. The means are an elaborate network of commissions, consultations among officials and elected representatives and programmes on regional and local levels. The range of activities has been extended following an initial programme of rural renovation, established by decree in October 1967, which covered one-third of all French farms.

The importance of technical information and training has long been appreciated, and a host of initiatives to promote '*la vulgarisation agricole*' have come from government, professional and private sources in the post-war period (see Houée, 1972, II, pp. 44–69). Efforts concentrated at first on encouraging the use of machinery and fertilizers to increase production. But the problem of encouraging a more sophisticated scientific–technical approach to farming, with an awareness of commercial and economic questions, was impeded by the very low educational levels prevailing. By 1960 only 7 per cent of farmers had the primary school certificate, and by 1975

*See Chapter 8 for a discussion of DATAR's central role in regional development.

only 10 per cent had received an element of formal training (*brevet d'apprentissage agricole*, or *certificat d'aptitude professionnelle agricole*). However, there was a strong tradition of informal oral and practical training, which expanded quite dramatically during the 1950s. Among the most important developments were the *Centres d'Etudes Techniques Agricoles* (CETA), which spread rapidly from 1955 and became 'intellectual co-operatives' for dynamic farmers. A high percentage of CETA members hold office in farm organizations and in local government. Another significant measure, influenced by the CETA movement, was the decree of April 1959 which gave the chambers of agriculture the means to develop their technical services by expanding the numbers of agricultural counsellors and advisers. By 1970 several hundred organizations, with 4500 technical advisers, were supported by the *Association Nationale pour le Développement Agricole* (ANDA). Its range of activities was further extended in 1973 by the creation of the *Fonds d'Assurance Formation pour les Exploitants Agricoles* (FAFEA). Although the objectives of the Seventh Plan to provide 50 per cent of farmers with formal training qualifications is extremely ambitious and is unlikely to be fulfilled, there is at least a reasonable prospect of progress towards that goal.

Other measures of importance in modernization involve group farming (*Groupements Agricoles d'Exploitation en Commun* – GAEC), producer groups (*groupement de producteurs*) and co-operatives. The first two were innovations of the 1960s, inspired by CNJA proposals. Although the numbers of joint farming ventures in the GAEC were not impressive at first, there has been rapid growth in recent years: from 3500 in 1973 to over 8000 in 1976. They are numerous in the regions of Brittany, Pays de la Loire, Rhône–Alpes, and Midi–Pyrénées. Their advantages are the sharing of capital costs, economies of scale and increased productive capacity. Meanwhile the number of producer groups (for example, producers of fruit, potatoes, eggs and chickens, wine, etc.), which are organized on a departmental and regional basis, have risen from 1000 in 1975 to nearly 1200 in 1977. They are numerous in the regions of Languedoc, Brittany, Aquitaine and Rhône–Alpes, but relatively scarce in the eastern regions, though efforts are being made to encourage them. Moreover, in accordance with the recommendations of a working party for the Sixth Plan (1971–5), '*inter-professional*' links are encouraged between producers and food-processing industries. The purpose is to maintain the quality of produce and to rationalize markets, but the discipline involved can be detrimental to the small, relatively inefficient producer who cannot attain the high standards required. The system works only if the groups can retain the loyalty of their members, so that the produce is marketed according to contractual obligations and not sold speculatively elsewhere when prices rise or withheld when prices fall. The temptation to speculate is strong, and the problem of disciplined marketing practices is far from being resolved. Nevertheless, these innovations are having an influence on Community marketing policy, and the Commission has shown an interest in encouraging their development.

In addition, producer co-operatives have contributed much to the improvement of marketing in France by dealing directly with wholesalers and large retail chains. Although the number of co-operatives is diminishing (from over 7000 in 1965 to under 5000 in the early 1970s), the volume of business has increased by an annual average of 21 per cent, and investments have more than doubled during that time. These figures refer to co-operatives, unions of co-operatives and *Sociétés d'Intérêt Collectif Agricole* (SICAs), which collect, prepare and market farm products, as well as supplying their members and providing them with technical advice. The largest number of co-operatives are in Alsace and the Mediterranean Midi, but the volume of business is much greater in the large-scale, streamlined organizations of the Paris Basin, Brittany and Upper Normandy. Co-operatives are preponderant among grain growers and are important in the dairy and wine sectors, but they are weak among meat producers.

The state plays an important role in the organization of

markets. By financing the establishment of *marchés d'intérêt national* in regions of production (Agen, Avignon, Montauban, Nantes, Nice, etc.) and in centres of consumption (Bordeaux, Lille, Lyon, Marseille, Strasbourg, etc.), it has aided the marketing of perishables. The centrepiece of the entire network is Paris–Rungis. On another level, that of market support, FORMA is a co-ordinating body under the supervision of the Ministries of Agriculture, Economy and Finance, which prepares governmental decisions concerning intervention in markets and is responsible for executing them. Since 1967 its function has extended to decisions taken in the framework of the Common Market. There are, in addition, a number of other public and semi-public bodies on which government representatives sit. The oldest of these is *L'Office National Interprofessionnel des Céréales* (ONIC), created in 1937 and reformed in 1963, which regulates the grain market. Its interventions are regulated in turn by Common Market procedures, but the nature of its activities – intervention buying, storage, the exporting and denaturing of grains – has not essentially changed. Its interventions are financed by the Guarantee section of the European Agricultural Guidance and Guarantee Fund, which is discussed below. There are similar bodies for sugar, potatoes, meat, wine, etc. Moreover, through *La Société pour l'Expansion des Ventes des Produits Agricoles et Alimentaires* (SOPEXA), the Ministry of Agriculture and the *Centre Français du Commerce Extérieur* have joined efforts with the various bodies to promote exports and domestic sales.

Although its proportion in the Gross Domestic Product has diminished from 13 per cent in 1954 to under 6 per cent in 1974, agriculture remains an essential economic activity. The value of total farm production was more than three times that of steel or textiles at 1974 prices, almost twice that of cars or electrical manufactures and much larger than that of the chemical industry. Moreover, the food-processing industry, in which the largest single branch (in terms of volume of business) is dairy products, ranks first in value of production and employs over half a million people. Exports of food and agricultural products accounted for 15–19 per cent of total exports in the period 1963–77. Although productivity in agriculture has progressively increased, it has remained behind the levels attained in other EEC countries. In terms of the contribution made by agriculture to Gross Domestic Product, France and Holland are comparable, with 5.7 per cent and 5.4 per cent respectively in 1974. In Holland, however, the agricultural sector represented 6.6 per cent of civilian employment, which was lower than France and indicated its greater farming efficiency. About a quarter of Holland's farm produce is exported, compared with somewhat less than a fifth for France. But the situation is not static, and the trends in France point towards greater concentration of farm land, more extensive market organization and continuing intense efforts to export.

THE COMMON AGRICULTURAL POLICY

One of the main achievements of the EEC was the creation of a Common Agricultural Policy (CAP), which came into effect in 1967. Its elaboration involved a series of marathon discussions about the detailed financial regulation of particular products. In January 1962 agreement was reached on the gradual organization of common markets for cereals, pork, poultry and eggs, fruit and vegetables, and wine. Agreements on other products followed in December 1964 and July 1966. The method of finance is the European Agricultural Guidance and Guarantee Fund, better known by its French initials as FEOGA. Most of the Fund, which represents about 75 per cent of annual Community expenditure and is by far the largest item of the Community budget, is spent on the Guarantee section. Its market-support operations include financing the costs of storing surpluses; subsidies and compensatory payments to producers arising from guaranteed prices; and export refunds, which cover the gap between higher Common Market prices and lower world prices. The benefits to French agriculture are beyond question: during the period 1962–74 France received over 36 per cent of the payments and contributed less than 26 per cent of the resources of the Fund. At the same time French farm exports to EEC partners boomed, and the favourable agricultural trade balance increased eightfold. The Guidance or *'Orientation'* section of the Fund encourages structural improvements in both production and marketing. But the financial agreement reached in 1966, at the conclusion of the French government's boycott of Community institutions, limited the scope of this section, in effect leaving farm modernization primarily to national governments. The agreement was reinforced in February 1970 by the West German government's insistence on restricting the budget of the Guidance section to 285 million units of account. The amount was increased by another 40 million units of account when the Community was enlarged to nine members; this is to be compared with the sum of 5500 million units of account allocated to the Guarantee section in 1976. The Commission's interest in farm modernization was shown in the Mansholt Plan published in December 1968, which was widely discussed and criticized (see *Revue du Marché Commun*, 1969; Rosenthal, 1975, pp. 24–6, 79–100). However, the revised 'mini-Mansholt' proposals of 1972, which owed much to the legislation of the Fifth Republic, were only very partially implemented by national governments, and structural policy has remained a national rather than a Community concern.

The prospect of enlarging the EEC to include Spain, Portugal and Greece has reopened the question of farm modernization. The active agricultural population in the original six member-countries was reduced from 16 million in 1958 to 7.5 million in 1975, but the entry of the three applicants would add another five million peasants. Moreover, their produce – wine, olive oil, fruit and vegetables – will merely add to the surpluses created by the southern farms of France and Italy. In the face of the potential competition, Mediterranean farmers have campaigned strongly for special aid from the EEC. The Commission responded in June 1978 with a 'Mediterranean package': a five-year programme of structural improvement and modernization for the Mediterranean regions of France and Italy. The measures, which cost the Community budget an extra £600 millions after approval by the Council of Ministers, include the financing of new rural infrastructures, afforestation, the improvement of vineyards, and support for processing and marketing projects and for the establishment of producer groups (EEC, 1978).

The package reflects the concern of the French government to make the Mediterranean farm sector more efficient, to enhance its market organization, to diversify production and to strengthen export capabilities. There is also an unexpressed concern to accomplish the transformation with a minimum of public disturbance by diffusing the impact of protests and demonstrations when they occur. Although the problems of Mediterranean agriculture have received much publicity because of the prospect of Community enlargement and the fears raised by it, they are, in fact, quite marginal (under 15 per cent of net farm output since 1975) to the overall position of French agriculture, which has shed much of its former backwardness and inefficiency. The FNSEA fully acknowledges the significant contribution of Community membership to the development of French agriculture as a whole:

> without the EEC, the situation of French agriculture would have been untenable and the tremendous expansion which it experienced in the past fifteen years would not have been realized ... the EEC permitted an increase in French agricultural prices; our prices were, for the most part, the lowest in Europe; European prices were fixed at a higher level ... between 1959 and 1975 French agricultural production increased by 61.3 per cent in volume and by 228 per cent in value. Where would our markets be without the EEC? The Community absorbed 28 per cent of our exports in 1959 and now absorbs 70 per cent. ... (FNSEA, 1976, pp. 158–9)

Although admitting that some agricultural sectors suffered heavily from foreign competition due to the opening of frontiers to Community partners and to 'certain advantages granted without sufficient consideration to third countries', as well as to exchange rate problems, criticisms of the Common Market are forcibly rejected as lies (*propos mensongers*). The attack is directed against 'politically motivated' groups which are not named, but evidently a major target is MODEF, the rival Communist-influenced organization, which recruits primarily among small farmers who are directly threatened by the patterns of change and who are adamantly hostile to the CAP and to the enlargement of the Community. The rivalry underlines the discrepancy between the 'two agricultures', which has been aggravated by the CAP because the main benefits do not accrue to the mass of the small peasantry. The Common Market represents, in fact, an opportunity only for the most competitive and best organized and is far from being a haven that permits the survival of 'family' farming (Delorme and Tavernier, 1969; Muth, 1970).

The long-standing demand of farm organizations for income parity with other sections of the economy was incorporated as a main goal of policy in the agricultural orientation law of August 1960. The relative success of such measures as the encouragement of retirement (IVD) and the regrouping of fragmented holdings has substantially increased average sizes of farms in many regions and has created a potential for higher incomes among the diminishing farm population. The conclusions reached by an INSEE study* is that the evolution of average farm income between 1956 and 1970 paralleled the average income of urban wage-earners. Disposable income in farm households, after deducting taxes and investment expenditures, was similar to that of employees and workers (see Table 4).

The level of disposable income for farmers was far behind that of even middle management, and so the demand for income parity was not attained in the fullest sense. But within agriculture, during the fifteen-year period, progress was made as primary incomes (derived directly from farming activities) were

---

*INSEE (1977). The measurement of farm income is complex because revenue derived from sources outside of agriculture (wages, rents, etc.) as well as transfer payments (of which social security benefits are the largest single item) have to be taken into account. To arrive at an estimate of disposable income, investment expenditures as well as taxes, have to be deducted.

TABLE 4   *Estimate of Disposable Income in 1970*

Socio-occupational category of head of household	Household index
Farmers	97
Farm labourers	68
Independent professions	185
Senior management and administration	203
Middle management and administration	127
Employees	93
Workers	88
Retired persons	64
Total ordinary households	100

Source: INSEE, *Les agriculteurs*, I (Paris: 1977), p. 168.

raised in value by 4.8 per cent a year and the value of transfer payments grew by 9.8 per cent a year.

However, the measurement of average income does not reveal the profound inequalities within agriculture that arise from differences in size of farms, type of activity and geographical location. In 1970 half of the gross farm income accrued to 27 per cent of the farms (which occupied 70 per cent of the available agricultural land). The difference between grain farming in the Paris Basin and peasant farming in the south is conveyed by the index of gross income per active family member (France = 100), which stood at 50 in Lozère and 543 in Seine-et-Marne in 1970. A report of the Ministry of Agriculture (INSEE, 1977, p. 187) distinguished three main groups:

(1) the 60,000 farms with incomes above the reference point (taken as the average gross non-agricultural earnings in the region or department) in 1972;

(2) the 275,000 farms with the potential for attaining parity, which could qualify for state aid on presentation of a detailed six-year plan of modernization, according to the terms of an EEC directive of April 1972;

(3) the 1,000,000 farms which could qualify for loans on less advantageous terms.

The drama of French agriculture is the future of the third

category. How many can survive in the 1980s? Of these, how many can hope to attain the threshold of viability necessary to qualify for state aid under the rigorous terms demanded by the EEC directive? It is clear that both the trends of change and the direction of policy bear out the evaluation of Mendras, who suggested that as agriculture modernizes and becomes integrated into the capitalist economy, traditional rural stratification would be replaced by a stratum of large and medium farmers, and the two other main groups – farm workers and peasantry – would become increasingly marginal in the social structure. The sharp decline in the numbers of farm workers (from over a million in 1954 to a third of that number in the 1970s) points to the existence of a scattered and weak group rather than to a rural working class parallel with urban labour. The small peasantry, surviving only by taking outside employment, is doomed to vanish. Sceptical of the idea that the revolutionary *élan* of the young peasants in the post-war period represented the formation of a peasant class, Mendras (1970, p. 245) underlined the degree to which 'the peasantry is moribund', and predicted that French farmers 'will be simply a professional group among others, with their own peculiarities and interests'.

The validity of the prediction is supported by the evidence presented in this chapter, but the persistence of long-standing traditions should not be overlooked. The objective or quantifiable socio-economic structures of farmingre changing rapidly, and the great myth of a separate world of rural values must necessarily dissolve. But agriculture is a colossal, permanent resource, a cornerstone of the French economy and a profound influence on the society; some, at least, of its traditional ethos will survive.

BIBLIOGRAPHY

BERGER, S. (1972) *Peasants Against Politics. Rural Organizations in Brittany* (Cambridge, Mass.: Harvard University Press).

BERGER, S. (1973) 'The French Political System', in S. H. Beer *et al.* (eds), *Patterns of Government*, 3rd edn (New York: Random House).

BOURRINET, J. (1975) 'Les incidences de la Politique Agricole Commune sur l'agriculture française', in J. Rideau *et al.* (eds), *La France et les communautés européennes* (Paris: LGDJ).

COLSON, R. (1977) *Un paysan face à l'avenir rural. La JAC et la modernisation de l'agriculture* (Paris: Editions de l'Epi).

DEBATISSE, M. (1963) *La révolution silencieuse: le combat des paysans* (Paris: Calmann-Lévy).

DELORME, H. (1975) 'La France et le Marché Commun Agricole', in Rideau *et al., op. cit.*

DELORME, H. and TAVERNIER, Y. (1969) *Les paysans français et l'Europe* (Paris: Presses de la Fondation Nationale des Sciences Politiques).

DE FARCY, H. (1975) *L'espace rural* (Paris: 'Que Sais-Je?').

EEC (1978) Background Report: 'Farm Policy Decisions 1978/9' (1 June).

FAUVET, J. and MENDRAS, H. (eds) (1958) *Les paysans et la politique dans la France contemporaine* (Paris: A. Colin).

FNSEA (1976) '30 ans de combat syndical' (March).

GERVAIS, M., JOLLIVET, M. and TAVERNIER, Y. (1976) *Histoire de la France rurale: la fin de la France paysanne, de 1914 à nos jours*, 4 vols (Paris: Seuil).

HOUEE, P. (1972) *Les étapes du développement rural*, 2 vols (Paris: Les Editions Ouvrières).

INSEE (1977) *Les agriculteurs*, 2 vols (E46–47).

JEGOUZO, G. (1972) *L'exode agricole*, Notes et Etudes Documentaires, La Documentation Française (3928).

JEGOUZO, G. and BRANGEON, J.-L. (1978) 'La condition sociale des petits paysans', in *Données sociales*, 3rd edn (Paris: INSEE).

KLATZMANN, J. (1972) *Geographie agricole de la France* (Paris: 'Que Sais-Je?').

LATIL, M. (1956) *L'évolution du revenu agricole* (Paris: Colin).

MALLET, S. (1962) *Les paysans contre le passé* (Paris: Seuil).

MENDRAS, H. (1959) *Sociologie de la campagne française* (Paris: 'Que Sais-Je?').

MENDRAS, H. (1970) *The Vanishing Peasant: Innovation and Change in French Agriculture* (Cambridge, Mass.: MIT Press).

MUTH, H. P. (1970) *French Agriculture and the Political Integration of Western Europe* (Leyden: Sijthoff).

Revue du Marché Commun (1969) 'L'agriculture européenne à un tournant' (November–December).

ROSENTHAL, G. (1975) *The Men Behind the Decisions* (Lexington, Mass.: D. C. Heath).

TAVERNIER, Y. (1969) *Le syndicalisme paysan* (Paris: FNSEA).

WRIGHT, G. (1968) *Rural Revolution in France* (Oxford: Oxford University Press).

CHAPTER 8

The Regional and Urban Setting

Martin Kolinsky

The dramatic social and economic changes of the post-war period were not experienced uniformly in the different regions of the country. The enormous concentration of economic activities in the Paris area was paralleled by under-development and under-utilization of capacities elsewhere. The lack of opportunities in the provinces accentuated the serious demographic imbalances in a period of vast migrations from agriculture. The unrestrained growth of Paris threatened to cause immeasurable social damage. Gravier's (1947) contrast between the congested gigantism of Paris and '*le désert français*' was in danger of becoming an irreversible reality. From the 1950s onwards, therefore, there were numerous policy initiatives designed to reduce the concentration of activities in the Paris area and to promote regional development (Monod and Castelbajac, 1971).

Reactions to the trends of change were by no means confined to planners and policy-makers. In certain areas a sense of regional consciousness found expression in liaison groups and in militant protest movements. The most vigorous of the former was the Breton *Comité d'Etudes et de Liaison des Intérêts Bretons* (CELIB), which was the first of the regional economic expansion committees created in the 1950s. The growth of autonomist movements in Corsica, Brittany (Phlipponeau, 1970) and Languedoc (the Occitan movement) was marked by some violent incidents, provoked by the efforts of these groups to press their claims. Discontent also surfaced in the relatively prosperous areas, notably Alsace, increasingly aware of the economic vigour and affluence of their Swiss and West German neighbours. The perception of prosperity elsewhere underlined a sense of deprivation and triggered demands for a more equitable distribution of economic resources and opportunities. Whether reinforced by protest demonstrations and bombings or not, these pressures posed two main types of problem for central government.

First, it was no longer a question, as it had been in the early post-war years, of setting targets for national recovery and economic growth without worrying about the lack of industry in the west and south. But to what extent could resources be diversified to the advantage of those regions without in effect penalizing the established industrial areas? Would the diffusion of effort weaken France in the face of intense international competition? The establishment of the Common Market, which exposed the French economy to harsh, competitive discipline, made the problem more difficult to resolve: to what extent does the desire for balanced and harmonious regional development contradict the need to reinforce developed regions in order to meet competition? Is it necessary to help Alsace and Lorraine at the expense of Poitou–Charentes and Limousin? The stubborn economic recession following the energy crisis of 1973–4 has made the dilemma more acute.

The second type of problem facing the government concerns the level of administrative change appropriate for the recognition, without loss of control, of the regional dimension of national problems. While the central government has *deconcentrated* some of its administrative powers in the regional reforms of 1964 and 1972 (see Chapter 4), it has done so with the intention of averting a more far-reaching *decentralization* of political power. It was recognized that the scale of modern economic activity undermined in many respects the usefulness of Napoleon's administrative divisions, but there was concern over the political consequences of change: the risk implied by the term 'region' is continual pressure for decentralization and autonomy, which could loosen the control of the unitary state and jeopardize the harmonization of central government objectives. Regional prefects were introduced in 1964, not as the backbone of a vigorous concept of regions, but minimally, as co-ordinators of existing departmental administrations. Nor was local democracy revitalized by the establishment of indirectly elected regional institutions: membership comprises parliamentary and other representatives and is constituted, to a limited extent, by appointment. The continuity of established local oligarchies and notables is thereby ensured.

Regions have been introduced, then, within the Napoleonic administrative framework, and they operate mainly within the terms of traditional local politics. However, the apparent triumph of the Jacobin state is to some extent conditional upon its capacity to promote urban and regional policies appropriate to a highly complex, differentiated and changing society. The question arises as to whether the outcome of such policies will be to strengthen the basis for an eventual decentralization of political power. Before considering this issue further, it will be useful to examine the process of urbanization and other significant changes, as well as the development of regional policy instruments.

URBANIZATION*

Compared with the development of urban environments in Britain and Germany, the rate and scope of urbanization in France was slow during the nineteenth century and the first half of the twentieth century. Whereas two-thirds of the British population lived in urban areas by 1870, as did over three-fifths of

---

*The focus here is on urbanization as a socio-economic pattern. See Wright (1978, Chapter 9) for a discussion of some of the political implications, such as the relative autonomy of the big towns and the role of mayors in the local–national political nexus.

the German population before the First World War, it was not until 1928 that the French population was evenly divided between urban and rural areas. Two basic factors account for this retardation: the slower rate and smaller scale of industrial development and a declining birth rate (which commenced in the nineteenth century with the widespread adoption of family limitation in France and was aggravated by the great losses of the First World War).

After the Second World War the trends were reversed. The birth rate increased dramatically, and from 1946 to 1968 the population grew by more than 9 million. Since 1968, however, population growth has slowed. The annual average growth of 1.2 per cent between 1962 and 1968, which includes the *rapatriés* from North Africa, fell to 0.8 per cent between 1968 and 1975 (immigration fell from 0.5 per cent to 0.2 per cent per annum, and natural increase from 0.7 per cent to 0.6 per cent). Simultaneous with the population growth was the massive exodus from agriculture and the great shift to secondary and tertiary occupations. The urban population increased from 25 million in 1954 to over 38 million in 1975 – that is, from 56 per cent of the total population to almost 75 per cent. The proportion is higher if the unit of measurement is changed from communes of 2000 or more inhabitants to urban zones (*zones de peuplement industriel ou urbain* – ZPIUs), in which a high proportion of people are gainfully occupied in non-agricultural activities and in which there is a high incidence of travelling to work in an urban setting. In 1962 over 77 per cent of the population lived in such zones, and the proportion rose to 83 per cent by 1975 – that is, nearly 44 million people. Twelve of the zones have more than 500,000 inhabitants. These are Paris (9.9 million), Lyon (1.4 million), Lille and Marseille (1 million each), Côte d'Azur (790,000), Bordeaux (755,000), *Bassin houiller ouest* (632,000), Toulouse (590,000), Strasbourg (560,000), *Bassin sidérurgique lorrain* (540,000), Rouen (523,000) and Saint-Etienne (522,000). Nantes, Nancy and Grenoble follow very closely.

Despite these recent developments, the pattern of urbanization remains distorted by the abnormal size of Paris, which is more than seven times greater than the second city, Lyon, and thirteen times greater than the fifth city, Bordeaux. In most other European countries the differences are much less pronounced. In his cogent study (1976, pp. 34, 36) Daniel Noin explains the pattern with reference to the administrative system:

> The relative weakness of the large provincial towns seems to be related both to the gigantism of the capital and to the great number of middle-sized towns; these two characteristics appear to be closely linked with the peculiarities of the French politico-administrative system ... the departments weakened the old regional capitals and spawned numerous middle-sized towns.

Paris has developed as the capital of France in every major sphere of activity. It is the political, administrative, cultural and scientific capital. Its sheer size is overwhelming, with nearly one-fifth of the total population concentrated into the Paris region, comprising 2 per cent of the national territory. Its influence as the centre of economic and political decision-making is felt in every nook and cranny of the country. The effect of the capital on the provinces has been much more profound than in other European countries, including Britain, where the influence of London has to some extent been balanced by other urban, industrial, political and cultural developments.* In France the attraction of Paris is the stronger in that such counterweights have been less pronounced (Ferniot, 1977).

Criticism of the crippling disadvantages of bureaucratic over-centralization and of an apoplectically congested capital is a time-honoured tradition. One of the most forceful expressions appeared in 1947, in Jean-François Gravier's book *Paris et le désert français*, which underlined the waste of resources in both economic and human terms. Coming at a time when the first plans for the restructuring and modernization of the French

---

*These include the political importance and strong manifestations of provincial life in the nineteenth century (Victorian civic pride) and the continuing significance of regional/national consciousness in Scotland, Wales and Northern Ireland.

economy were being established, the book had considerable influence. It was increasingly acknowledged that the modernization of France involved both control over the growth of Paris and the development of provincial economies. After decades of neglect, the need for urban planning was keenly felt, and the value of regional development was perceived.

The *Plan d'Aménagement et d'Organisation Générale de la Région Parisienne* (PADOG) was adopted in 1960. Its intention was to reduce the flow of migration into the region from over 100,000 a year to 50,000. An act restricting the extension of office and industrial premises was passed. In 1964 the departments of the region were reorganized. The former Seine and Seine-et-Oise departments were replaced by seven new departments; Seine-et-Marne remained unchanged. By this time it was apparent that the aims of PADOG could not be realized without stricter controls and a more realistic appraisal of the means necessary for reducing the urban concentration. In 1965 the *Schéma Directeur d'Aménagement et d'Urbanisme* was authorized by the regional prefect, Delouvrier. Instead of rejecting the overspill towns as the original plan had done, it provided for the creation of five new towns along two axes (Melun–Mantes and Meaux–Pontoise). In addition to adopting PADOG's designs for suburban redevelopment, the blueprint planned a transport system based on new motorways and a regional express *métro*. The *Schéma Directeur* was revised in 1969, after the administrative services of the region were organized and the duties of the regional prefect laid down; it was revised again in 1975, though the fundamental concepts are intact. Among the many important developments were the transfer of Les Halles food market to Rungis in 1969, the completion of the ring road, Boulevard Périphérique, in 1972, the opening of Charles de Gaulle airport at Roissy in 1974, the launching of thirty development schemes in 1971 and the overall transport development plan of 1972.

While these developments were being planned, a broader attack on the problem was conceived: the idea of designating eight large provincial cities as *métropoles d'équilibre*, or counterweights to the excessive predominance of the capital (Lyon, Marseille, Lille, Toulouse, Bordeaux, Nantes, Strasbourg and Nancy). To promote their development *Organisations d'Etudes d'Aménagement d'Aires Métropolitaines* (OREAMs) were set up in 1965 in Marseille–Aix, Lille–Roubaix–Tourcoing, Nantes–St-Nazaire, Lyon–Saint Etienne–Grenoble, Nancy–Metz–Thionville and the Basse Vallée de la Seine. They are under the control of the inter-ministerial planning committee (CIAT). Five more were added in subsequent years: Picardie, Centre, Bordeaux–Aquitaine, Strasbourg–Région Alsace; Toulouse–Region Midi–Pyrénées (the latter was short-lived because local agreement about its aims and methods could not be obtained).

Gravier, in his updated reflexions (1972) expressed dissatisfaction with the tendency of the first OREAMs (except Lille) to aim for large-scale growth. He thought that they would

> introduce a division, deplorable in every respect, between a privileged zone and the rest of the region in which they seem not to be interested. It is a separation all the less justified in that the '*aires métropolitaines*' incorporate worker agglomerations which had never anything in common with a metropolis. It took several years of reflexion before the authorities at DATAR came to write: 'The metropolitan areas should be defined by their role rather than by their mass.'

In some respects this judgement is too harsh because during the first decade, 1966–76, the OREAMs developed broader objectives. To begin with their role was to establish *schémas directeurs* for the metropolitan areas and to define the means of action for the realization of the plans, after approval by the CIAT. By the early 1970s, however, the OREAMs were extending their interests to regional plans for transport and communications, tourism, studies of the relationship of urban and rural environments, middle-sized towns and strategies for economic development.* After the regional reforms of 1972 the

---

*Examples of such strategies include the *Centre méditerranéen de commerce international* in the Marseille region, the mining and coastal areas in the Nord and the plan for the Massif Vosgien prepared jointly by the OREAMs of Lorraine and Alsace and the *Mission Régionale* of Franche-Comté.

OREAMs increasingly developed into bodies for regional study and planning activities (for example, associating the state, local public authorities and private enterprise in the creation of industrial sites and other infrastructures). This is a tendency rather than a systematic pattern; the original objectives remain primary, which explains why twelve of the twenty-two regions do not have such institutions. Nevertheless, five OREAMs were transformed into regional study organizations for the whole of the Nord, Picardie, Centre, Aquitaine, Provence–Alpes–Côte d'Azur and Strasbourg. The brief from the start was for the whole of Alsace, though local rivalries have, in fact, limited it to the department of Bas-Rhin. The enlargement of functions was confirmed in two circulars issued in March 1973 and February 1974 by Olivier Guichard, Minister of MATELT (Ministre de l'Aménagement du Territoire, de l'Equipement, du Logement et du Tourisme). The circulars stressed that as organs of inter-ministerial competence, the OREAMs are involved in *national* regional policy as well as regional and inter-regional development. Moreover, the circulars emphasize that although it is desirable for the OREAMs to co-operate with the *Etablissement Public Territorial* under the control of the regional councils, they are nevertheless *administrative bodies* responsible to the regional prefect and under the administrative control of the *Chef du Service Régional de l'Equipement*. But so far from being stifled, the OREAMs are buzzing with ideas and proposals which makes them important centres of research, planning and co-ordination. OREAM–Aquitaine, for example, initiated a project with the *Chambre Régionale de Commerce et d'Industrie d'Aquitaine* which aims to multiply economic and cultural links with Africa "in order to 'sell' the region, so that it may be perceived as a privileged European partner . . .".

REGIONAL POLICY

The establishment of regional structures and the development of policy is recorded in a series of decrees and planning documents.

The decrees of 30 June 1955 were important in several respects, as they defined state aids for industrial relocation and conversion, created the *Fonds de Développement Economique et Social*, and established a significant planning instrument, the *Société de Développement Régional*, which is discussed below. At the same time the principle of establishing regional action programmes was decreed, which led to the publication in the following years of plans delineating the socio-economic characteristics of regions and to proposals for solving their problems. In 1965 twenty-two economic planning regions were created, grouping together various departments whose administrative boundaries were maintained. Since regional planning activities affected various ministries – Finance, Public Works and Transport, Industry, Agriculture and the Interior (especially the prefects) – the need for co-ordination was increasingly felt, and late in 1960 an inter-ministerial committee was established. In February 1963 it became the *Délégation à l'Aménagement du Territoire et à l'Action Régionale* (DATAR), which may be roughly translated as the 'agency for territorial development and regional action', working for the Prime Minister, Georges Pompidou. It was later (June 1974) placed under the authority of the Ministry of the Interior and then returned to the Prime Minister's office after the March 1978 elections.

DATAR is a central focus of regional policy initiatives. It has two prime functions, of which one is the co-ordination of policy among the ministries and, through the regional prefect, at regional and departmental levels. One of its most important means of achieving this is the regionalization of the state capital expenditure budget. The annual report, in the preparation of which the regional prefects participate, makes it possible to follow the achievement of priority objectives. DATAR also has considerable innovative impact through its development of specialized administrative bodies: the OREAMs; commissions for the rural renovation of Brittany, Auvergne, Limousin and mountain areas; commissions for industrial development of the Atlantic and Mediterranean seaboards and for the industrial restructuring of Lorraine and the Nord; inter-ministerial missions for the promotion of tourism in Aquitaine, Languedoc–Roussillon and Corsica; and, in an effort to attract foreign investments, it has established offices in New York, Frankfurt, Tokyo, London, Stockholm, Berne, Madrid and the Persian Gulf. DATAR has also co-operated with INSEE in setting up regional *Observatoires Economiques* to collect and distribute economic and social information. DATAR is closely involved with a number of important special bodies: the Decentralization Committee, which processes applications for opening or extending premises in the Paris region; the Inter-ministerial Group for Land (GIF), which establishes state guidelines for land reserves; the Economic and Social Fund (FDES), which grants subsidies and loans to attract firms to priority regions; and the National Commission for Regional Development (CNAT), which is concerned with long-term policy.

In addition to participation in the FDES, DATAR has its own Intervention Fund for Regional Development (FIAT), which is about 1 per cent (about 300 million francs) of the state's investment budget. The fund is used for launching schemes which are then taken over by the technical ministries. Although small in itself, the fund has a pump-priming role and can mobilize a large portion of state capital works financing. It has been used principally for road building.

The term 'region' was first used in official texts in decrees of March 1964 (which DATAR helped to prepare) announcing the appointment of regional prefects and establishing regional consultative bodies (CODERs). The word was out, despite previous fears of raising a problem which could not be solved, but its substance was limited. Louis Joxe, then Minister of State in charge of administrative reform, did not risk upsetting the partisans of traditional state centralization too much in declaring: 'The region is not to be a new administrative echelon. It cannot and should not become a new *collectivité locale*. It is a relay between the central power and the department' (quoted in Abrial, 1974, p. 7). There was clearly no intention of diminishing the role of the department. In fact, the regional prefect was chosen from among the departmental prefects and continued to be in charge of a department. But he was given wider responsibilities, including that of preparing the regional section of the national plan. To carry out his new role, the regional prefect was provided with a staff of senior civil servants.

As discussed in Chapter 4, the consultative body, CODER, was not elected but consisted of mayors, departmental councillors, representatives of interest groups and prefectoral nominees. Its role was principally the preparation of the regional section of the national plan, but in practice its influence proved to be very limited. This led to much disillusionment, which was intensified later by the attempt of de Gaulle to use the regional issue as a means of reinforcing his personal prestige in the aftermath of the 1968 crisis. The rejection of the April 1969 referendum on regional reform and reform of the Senate led to de Gaulle's resignation. His proposals were far-reaching, particularly the extent of financial autonomy he envisaged and his definition of the juridical status of regions as *collectivités territoriales*, which would have placed them on an equal footing with the departments. When regional reforms were subsequently implemented after the law of July 1972, it was not long before the economic climate deteriorated. The energy crisis, threatening inflation and rising unemployment overshadowed the longer-term questions of structural change. The administrative map of France was changed, with the introduction of twenty-two regions in which the regional prefect is flanked by a *conseil régional* (consisting of parliamentarians and delegates from the departmental *conseils généraux*, municipal councils and urban communities) and a *comité économique et social*. The limited nature of the changes have been underscored by commentators who prefer directly elected councils, greater financial resources and autonomy and less dependence on the regional (and, indeed, departmental) prefects. Some would like to see larger and more powerful regions, perhaps twelve in number, representing a genuine decentralization of power; a few seek that anathema of the unitary state – federalism. What was in fact established was little more than administrative deconcentration, almost wholly devoid of political responsibility. The role of the regions is restricted to the co-ordination of the activities of the departments and the communes in the field of regional development (Dulong, 1978; Irving, 1975).

There are also a number of important public (though non-governmental) bodies with close links with the administration, which are deeply involved in problems of regional development – most notably the *Chambres de Commerce et d'Industrie*, the *Chambres d'Agriculture*, and the *Sociétés de Développement Régional* (SDR). Whereas the first two have been established since the 1920s, the latter is a much more recent and novel institution. The first Monnet Plan directed its efforts towards the reconstruction and modernization of basic industries, with the effect that middle-sized firms, particularly in the provinces, suffered from a shortage of credit facilities. To overcome the problem, Pierre Pflimlin, then Minister of Finance and Economic Affairs, established a new institution, the SDR, by a decree of June 1955. The SDRs are private companies (*sociétés anonymes*) with a special legal status. On the advice of the executive council of the FDES, the Ministry of Finance and Economic Affairs (since April 1978 it has been divided into two ministries) enters into agreement with each of the SDRs providing a dividend guarantee and fiscal exemptions and designating a commissioner of the government who is a member of the SDR's board and attends shareholder meetings. The other members of the board are the usual array of economic notables: representatives of the participating banks and financial institutions, presidents of the chambers of commerce and industry, representatives of local industries, etc. Moreover, the directors of the SDRs are in close contact with the prefects, the regional planning organizations and committees and inspectors (from the state economics ministries), so that their activity is in accordance with the various programmes of regional development.

Pflimlin, later mayor of Strasbourg, was deeply involved in regional problems, and the first SDR to sign its agreement with the Ministry was in Alsace in March 1956. It was closely followed by the *Société Lorraine de Développement et d'Expansion* (Lordex) and by its equivalent in Nord and Pas-de-Calais. Before the end of 1960 twelve more SDRs were established, covering the whole of France except for the Paris region. By 1 October 1964 more than a thousand million francs had been lent to over 1200 firms for the creation of 86,000 jobs. Although their capital resources were meagre to start with – subscribed from banking, regional industries and local savings institutions – there was signficant reinforcement in the early 1960s through the participation of the *Crédit National* and again in 1974 by state guaranteed loans. Since 1975 the state has increasingly taken the initiative, so that, to a certain extent, the SDRs are becoming agencies for the distribution of state credits. However, their financial resources are by no means limited, and apart from various French sources, some of them draw occasionally on the European Investment Bank as well as from capital markets in other European countries and abroad. Moreover, SDRs may join forces to raise capital for certain purposes, a practice developed by the four SDRs in the east – Lordex, Sade (Alsace), Champex (Champagne–Ardenne) and Centrest (Bourgogne, Franche-Comté, Nivernais). During the twenty-year period to 1976 the SDRs provided over ten thousand million francs to more than 5000 firms.

The role of an SDR is not limited to the provision of credit. It becomes involved with the firms as financial adviser and consultant on modernizing structures. The SDRs have developed two services of value for the latter: *France-Cadres*, for the recruitment and training of *cadres*, and the *Centre Interrégional de Négociation*, which facilitates contractual agreements between firms in different regions. The SDRs are, therefore, the planning instruments most closely involved with the internal activities and decisions of local firms. This is undoubtedly a considerable achievement, which contributes much to the policy of diversifying regional industries. Nevertheless, their field of action is circumscribed. In Lorraine, for example, some 890 projects have been financed in the twenty-year period, but it has involved only 440 medium-sized firms. One of the directors of Lordex stressed that much more could have been done but for the scarcity of good projects and competent people. He was emphatic that the problem was not a lack of financial means. He pointed out (in an interview with MK, 24 November 1977) that 'the head of a small firm is either a businessman or a manager or a technician. He is rarely all three at once, and it is difficult for him to understand that he has to find people capable of filling the other functions once his enterprise has reached a certain size.' Although the situation is similar in other parts of France such as Aquitaine, the SDRs are developmental instruments which have proved their worth and are likely to become more significant in the future. They serve as a vital link with small and medium-sized firms exhibiting innovative and adaptive capacities.

In addition to these developments, the plans for economic modernization have given some attention to regional problems. The Second Plan (1954–7) was concerned to help regions with declining industries and to stimulate the industrialization of agricultural regions with a high population density, particularly in the west. The Third Plan (1958–61) devoted a chapter to the analysis of regional disparities and the excessive concentration on Paris. In 1963 CNAT, which links the planning commissariat and DATAR, was created to establish long-term regional objectives for the Fifth and subsequent plans. Given the multiplicity of problems to be tackled, it has proven difficult to avoid some contradictions in the attempt to meet them. For example, regions in the west, the south-west and the Massif Central have been given priority in order to transform their agricultural economies, provide new industrial jobs and raise income levels. The results are an increase, between 1962 and 1974, of the order of 40 per cent in the number of industrial jobs in the west (from 1,182,000 to 1,637,000), with a decline of 5 per cent in the Paris region during the same period (from 1,388,000 to 1,305,000). The regional disparities in average income levels (net income per capita) have tended to diminish to a certain extent. However, the crises afflicting the textile, mining and steel industries, which created rising unemployment in the zones of conversion in the north and east, have made the task of diversifying more urgent. Under such pressures the tendency is to multiply special programmes and administrative bodies, which results in both confusion and a dilution of aims because incentives cannot apply effectively everywhere; not everything can be a priority.*

CNAT's second report, relevant to the regional section of the Sixth Plan (1971–5), took account of several changes which had become apparent by the end of the 1960s. First, certain major objectives were being only partially realized: the industrialization of western regions was proceeding at a very moderate rate; the eight *métropoles d'équilibre* were not developing strongly enough to counterbalance the predominance of Paris. Secondly, European competition was felt keenly both at national level and in the border regions. Thirdly, there was increasing recognition of the importance of tertiary or service-sector employment in job creation and in establishing stable urban environments outside Paris. Finally, environmental issues emerged with some force and conflicted to an extent with strictly 'economic' preoccupations with raising material standards of living. But, before the Sixth Plan had run its course, the world economic situation had changed dramatically, and the Seventh Plan (1976–80) had to consider its economic and social objectives against a background of crisis and in the face of a period of risk and grave uncertainty.

The three main aspects of regionalism in France are administrative deconcentration, regional planning and diffuse aspirations for a viable level of intermediate government. The 1964 reforms created the most visible sign of the former – regional prefects – and gave some substance to the latter in the form of CODER advisory bodies. The 1972 reform continued along the same lines, endowing the twenty-two regions with a status below that of the departments and communes,

*Alduy report, *Commission des Finances, de l'Economie Générale et du Plan*, Assemblée Nationale, 16 novembre 1978, No. 570, pp. 28ff.

which are *collectivités territoriales*. The legal status of the regions as *établissements publics* is intermediate between the normal reference of French administrative law to a public institution, such as state schools, and the *collectivités territoriales*. The region is one of a number of territorial *établissements publics – communautés urbaines, syndicats de communes* – which group together various *collectivités territoriales* for certain common undertakings. The regions were established as a framework of '*concertation*' among existing authorities, and the implication that they might become a basis for political decentralization or devolution was firmly rejected. But demands for greater initiative and responsibility at local levels continued to be raised.

Although the Guichard report on the development of local responsibilities (*Vivre Ensemble*, 1976) did not attempt to deal with the political aspect of regionalism, it did foresee the possibility that a new intermediate level of government could be developed between the state and a renovated municipal network by merging the departments and the existing regions. The report has been shelved by the government and is unlikely to serve as a basis for local and regional government reforms (see Machin, 1978). It is, therefore, not surprising that some very harsh judgements have been delivered on the situation. For example, the *Le Monde* specialist on regions, François Grosrichard, wrote in the issue of 15 February 1978: 'Regionalization is without doubt a legal reality, with the reform of 1972, but it remains *une fiction politique*. Similarly decentralization to the departments or communes remains an illusion.' A further limitation is the concentration of economic decision-making. An economist, Maurice Marchand-Tonel, recognizing that French governments regard regionalization as politically suspect, has pointed out that the policy of industrial decentralization is little more than rhetoric as far as the centres of decision-making are concerned. He notes that a number of important enterprises controlled by the state, including Air Inter, have maintained their headquarters in Paris and that there is a continuing process of suction which forces the larger provincial firms to establish their headquarters in the capital: 'Without the example of real decentralization by the state, the important centres of private decision-making cannot avoid becoming more and more Parisian' (*Le Monde*, 25 January 1978).*

Although these judgements emphasize the severe constraints within which regional policy operates, it does not mean that the initiatives undertaken since the 1950s are unsuccessful or without consequence. The initial policy of trying to develop a more balanced social economy meant reducing the concentration of economic activities in the Paris area. Results were not immediately forthcoming, but the 1968 census showed the beginnings of a reversal of long-term trends. The growth of the Paris region had slowed; population exchanges with the provinces were becoming more balanced (departures from Paris to the provinces were nearing the number of arrivals – 109,000 departures per year as compared with 120,000 arrivals per year for the period 1962–8); and most of the larger provincial cities (except Lille) had a faster growth rate than Paris. These trends were confirmed in the 1975 census. The positive migration balance is a constant and moderating element in the growth of the Paris region, while the *unités urbaines* of Lyon, Marseille and Lille grew relatively more rapidly than the Paris agglomeration. Moreover, the regions of the west (Pays de la Loire, Bretagne and Poitou–Charentes) experienced more rapid demographic growth than in the preceding census period (INSEE, 1977, pp. 24, 30, 33).

In addition to the urban schemes (*métropoles d'équilibre*, new towns and the more recent concern to strengthen the capacity for development of middle-sized towns), a number of other initiatives have been sponsored by the inter-ministerial bodies which operate alongside the traditional administrations. These schemes include big industrial projects such as the Fos complex near Marseille, the Toulouse aerospace centre and the Lower

---

*The Vasseur report (1979, p. 21) indicates that 375 of the 500 top firms had their headquarters in the Paris region in 1958. This increased to 388 in 1976, whereas over the same period the numbers decreased in the Rhône–Alpes region (which includes Lyon, St.-Etienne and Grenoble) from 20 to 15.

Seine Valley Development Plan; tourist development areas; and rural renovation plans. The list of efforts is impressive, and there are some positive results. State aid in priority regions from 1956 to 1973 is estimated to have established a total of 350,000 jobs. The most significant period was 1969–73, which accounts for over 60 per cent of the expenditure and jobs created. In terms of the latter, the chief beneficiaries during this period were Nord (30,000 jobs), Pays de la Loire (over 25,000), Bretagne (nearly 23,000), Lorraine (over 20,000), and Aquitaine and Poitou (nearly 20,000 each). In addition, more than 2000 firms in priority regions benefited from state aid between 1964 and 1975 for technical training of some 200,000 workers. That is far from the whole story. Between 1955 and 1973 the FDES granted nearly 900 long-term loans (at low rates of interest) to promote regional industrial expansion, quite apart from a range of fiscal advantages offered to firms willing to establish themselves in, or to expand into, designated areas (Durand, 1974, pp. 87–99). To appreciate the scale of the efforts, one has to add to these amounts the investments and credits allocated through the regionalization of the national budget, the pump-priming effects of FIAT, the investment loans made available through the SDRs and various kinds of aid from local collectivities and local bodies (Monod, 1974).

Undoubtedly a measure of *industrial* decentralization has been achieved, with the transfer of about 500,000 jobs since the mid-1950s,* though the tendency to remain within 200 kilometres of the capital is pronounced. A more serious limitation is that a large proportion of the jobs created (particularly in the western regions) are low-skilled, the intention of many firms being to exploit the availability of relatively cheap labour rather than to become integrated into the regional economy (Astorg, 1975, II, p. 331; see also Chardonnet, 1976, III, pp. 374–8). In these cases the headquarters and main production units remain in the Paris area (the nationalized Renault motor company, for

---

*Total industrial employment in the Paris region increased from 1,370,000 in 1954 to 1,388,000 in 1962, then declined to 1,305,000 in 1974. The figures do not include employment in building and public works.

example). More serious still is the almost nugatory decentralization of tertiary occupations: half of the office space created in
France between 1965 and 1971 was located in the Paris region,
where over a quarter of national tertiary employment is found.
Little change may be expected as long as both economic and
political decision-making are concentrated in Paris and governments continue to be reluctant to undertake more than token
measures of decentralization with respect to their own administrations and the state-controlled enterprises.

Paris also holds the purse-strings. Given the inter-ministerial
nature of regional policy and the involvement of central, departmental and local authorities, an evaluation of the total sums
involved is difficult. In the early 1970s more than a thousand
million francs were directly committed, and several times that
amount were spent on improving infrastructures; expenditure
rose steadily during the decade. By contrast, the budgets controlled by the regional authorities themselves are small. The
range is from under 24 million francs in Limousin (740,000 population) in 1978 to 283 millions in Rhône–Alpes (4,660,000
population). The size is indicative of the political insignficance of
regionalism, though the budgets are not without relevance for
certain types of expenditure, notably communications, rural
development and cultural activities. This reflects the essential
activities of the regions: the co-ordination of local authority
investments and the drawing together of neighbouring departments and communes in planning exercises.

Compared with the bolder visions of regional autonomy, the
system introduced by the 1972 law is greatly restricted and is
perfectly in line with the traditional bureaucratic ethos of central
government. The question that is implicit in the operation of
the regional institutions is whether new political demands
for participation – elected regional assemblies with greater
powers – may be eventually generated. The question would
perhaps have been posed more urgently in the late 1970s if the
economic recession following the energy crisis had not brought
such a change in the climate of concern: inflation, unemployment, trade deficits, low growth of production. Nevertheless, the

value placed on development in all regions, the diffuse desires for decentralization and democratic participation, the existence of some regional movements and the increasing volume of information about regional problems all combine to make it a potentially live issue (though a well-worn doctrine) and to make regional policy a focus of continuing interest (Tarrow *et al.*, 1978). Undoubtedly, the contrast between political rhetoric and the unbending reality of highly centralized economic and political decision-making aggravates a strongly developed sense of disillusionment in some quarters. But given the vastness of the socio-economic changes which are transforming the country to create a new urban France, it is hard to imagine that Napoleonic traditions will merely continue to survive indefinitely. After all, regional reform was introduced to provide the means of co-ordination – 'a relay', in the words of the minister responsible, 'between the central power and the department' – which was widely perceived to be lacking. The departments were too narrow a framework for developmental purposes. What remains to be determined (see *Vasseur Rapport*, 1979, p. 45; Watson, 1978) is the relative importance regions may acquire in the search for that cherished goal: the harmonious and balanced development of economy and society.

BIBLIOGRAPHY

ABRIAL, P. (1974) *La réforme régionale: loi du 5 juillet 1972*, Notes et Etudes Documentaires, La Documentation Française (4064).

ASTORG, M. (1975) 'Le développement régional et l'aménagement du territoire', *Profil économique de la France*, Vol II, Notes et Etudes Documentaires, La Documentation Française (4245–8).

CHARDONNET, J. (1976) *L'économie française*, 4 vols (Paris: Dalloz).

DULONG, R. (1978) *Les régions, l'Etat et la société locale* (Paris: PUF).

DURAND, P. (1974) *Industrie et régions: l'aménagement industriel du territoire*, 2nd edn, La Documentation Française.

FERNIOT, J. (1977) *C'est ça la France* (Paris: Julliard).

GRAVIER, J.-F. (1947) *Paris et le désert français* (Paris: Flammarion).

GRAVIER, J.-F. (1970) *La question régionale* (Paris: Flammarion).

GRAVIER, J.-F. (1972) *Paris et le désert français en 1972* (Paris: Flammarion).

GREMION, P. (1976) *Le pouvoir périphérique* (Paris: Seuil).

GREMION, P. and WORMS, J.-P. (1968) *Les institutions régionales et la société locale* (Paris: Copedith).

INSTITUT FRANCAIS DES SCIENCES ADMINISTRATIVES (1978) *Le région en question?* (Paris: Cujas).

INSEE (1976) *Pour situer l'Alsace* (Strasbourg).

INSEE (1977) *Principaux résultats du recensement de 1975*.

INSEE (annual) *Statisques et indicateurs des régions françaises*.

IRVING, R. E. M. (1975) 'Regionalism in France', in J. Cornford (ed.), *The Failure of the State* (London: Croom Helm).

KAYSER, B. and KAYSER, J.-L. (1971) *95 régions*. . . . (Paris: Seuil).

MACHIN, H. (1978) 'All Jacobins Now? The Growing Hostility to Local Government Reform', *West European Politics* (October), 133–150.

MONOD, J. (1974) *Transformation d'un pays* (Paris: Fayard).

MONOD, J. and CASTELBAJAC, Ph. de (1971) *L'aménagement du territoire* (Paris: 'Que Sais-Je?').

NOIN, D. (1976) *L'espace français* (Paris: Colin).

PFLIMLIN, P. and UHRICH, R. (1963) *L'Alsace: destin et volonté* (Paris: Calmann–Lévy).

PHLIPPONEAU, M. (1970) *Debout Bretagne!* (Rennes: Presses Universitaires de Bretagne).

PISANI, E. (1969) *La région . . . pour quoi faire?* (Paris: Calmann–Lévy).

SERVAN-SCHREIBER, J.-J. (1971) *Le pouvoir régional* (Paris: Grasset).

TARROW, S., KATZENSTEIN, P. J., and GRAZIANO, L. (eds) (1978) *Territorial Politics in Industrial Nations* (New York: Praeger).

THOENIG, J.-C. and DANSEREAU, F. (1968) *Le société locale face à une institution nouvelle d'aménagement du territoire: le cas de la métropole d'équilibre Lorraine* (Paris: CNRS).

UHRICH, R. (1977) *Pour une économie alsacienne réconciliée* (Colmar: Alsatia).

VASSEUR Rapport (1979) *Avis et rapports du Conseil Economique et Social* (JO 12 January).

WALLACE, H. (1977) 'The Establishment of the Regional Development Fund', in H. Wallace, W. Wallace and C. Webb (eds), *Policy-making in the European Communities* (London: Wiley).

WATSON, M. (1978) 'A Critique of Development From Above. The Lessons of French and Dutch Experience of Nationally Defined Regional Policy', *Public Administration* (Winter), 457–81.

WRIGHT, V. (1978) *The Government and Politics of France* (London: Hutchinson).

CHAPTER 9

Persistent Cleavages in a Changing Society: An Overview

*Michalina Vaughan**

French society cannot be studied without reference to the history which shaped its structures and in which its culture is steeped.† This point does not amount to an endorsement of historical determinism: it is merely a recognition that knowledge of the past is a precondition for understanding the present. Without such knowledge, contemporary reality is so manifold and fast-changing that it appears meaningless. Even an attempt at description rather than evaluation entails a more or less explicit reliance on historical material, which provides a template for the selection of relevant features and a guide to the detection of trends. Indeed, the complexity of an advanced society makes it essential to choose from among the bewildering variety of its aspects and the mass of data available on each of them. The search for analogies and contrasts with the past provides criteria whereby this choice is made – in somewhat

*Thanks are due to Dr Peta Sheriff for contributing ideas and material towards this chapter.
†Either a Marxist or a structural-functionalist approach would emphasize the structural origins of culture, as a response to societal needs. By contrast, an interplay of structure and culture is posited here, in the tradition of Weberian sociology.

189

impressionistic fashion by all thinking individuals, more systematically and more consciously by the social scientist. In either case, the approach to contemporary society is through comparisons over time. Patterns of continuity and change can thus be found, and contradictory information about societal characteristics can be ordered along these lines. The most elementary statements, including those which define such a society as 'advanced' or complex, are based on a comparative approach. Terms of comparison are sought either over time (in relation to a traditional, allegedly simpler past) or in space (by drawing parallels between societies at various stages of development).

Statements about the extensiveness of social change experienced in France since the end of the Second World War are derived from a posited contrast between past and present. To acknowledge that such a contrast exists is not an ideological tenet or a value-judgement. In France agreement on this point can be found between supporters of the ruling majority, who claim that the political stability achieved under the Fifth Republic has provided the necessary framework for structural reforms, and by their most determined opponents, for whom the regime is an obstacle to a global restructuring of the economy and of stratification. Thus according to Jean Ellenstein, the eminent intellectual of the Communist Party: 'France has changed more – this is commonplace – in the last thirty years than in the previous century and a half' (*Le Monde*, 22 November 1977). There is no difficulty in supplying demographic and economic statistics in support of this widely shared view.

DEMOGRAPHIC CHANGE

Having stagnated for over a century, the French population increased nearly twice as much in the twenty years following the end of the Second World War as in the previous hundred (Dyer, 1978). After the baby boom of the mid-1940s, the subsequent steady rate of growth, on a scale unprecedented in the country's history, was totally unexpected. It was due both to a high birth rate, which only began to decline in 1963 and picked up again in the mid-seventies (14.1 per thousand), and to a steady decline in the mortality rate, which stabilized in the late sixties at about 10.5 per thousand. While the latter phenomenon can be attributed to medical progress and higher living standards, the causes of the former are somewhat more elusive. It is unclear to what extent financial inducements to increase family size influenced behaviour and, hence, whether the 'natalist' policy of the state (maternity allowances, family allowances, social legislation) was effective. Attitudinal changes in such matters are notoriously difficult to explain. In the short run, such variables as the return of prisoners of war, the planned postponement of births in wartime (and possibly even during the previous period of economic depression) and the mere fact of return to normality must have had some impact. At any rate, a demographic renewal started and, despite some official disappointment at the fact that the post-war bulge resulted in a very small upswing in natality in the mid-seventies, the decrease in fecundity during the current decade has been smaller in France than in any other Western European country, Italy included.

From the late 1950s onwards demographic change had far-reaching socio-economic implications. The most striking repercussions were felt within the educational system, as it began to cope with the so-called '*explosion scolaire*'. In 1963–4 the number of primary pupils was 69 per cent higher than the annual average for the years 1945–50. Secondary (*lycée*) intakes trebled in fifteen years. The demand for tertiary education underwent a commensurate increase, and recording these numerical pressures helps to account for the university crisis which triggered off the events of 1968. Educational establishments designed for a small elite were not prepared to impart mass education. Yet a premium was put on formal qualifications for employment within an economy in which the tertiary sector expanded at the expense of secondary and, mostly, of primary occupations. Thus the educational system underwent strong and contradictory pressures – to expand and to diversify, to maintain standards of excellence (somewhat rigidly defined within a centralized system) and to provide vocational training for a fast-changing occupational structure. The long record of centrally designed reforms, generally resisted by teaching staffs and withdrawn before their impact had been truly felt, culminated in what, at the time, could almost be called a revolution. It seems obvious, with hindsight, that unrest escalated from the university to the streets of Paris because the young outside the academic sphere were also dissatisfied with, and frustrated by, many aspects of a society designed for a smaller and older population. The lack of housing, persistently denounced by the economist Alfred Sauvy as the fundamental failure of the French economy in the post-war years, was one such irritant. The excessive growth of the Paris area at the expense of western and central France (so that in 1968 only 51 per cent of the Parisian population was actually born there) was another source of overcrowding and discontent. The concern for 'quality of life' – as an alternative to growth – became one of the *leit motivs* of protest in 1968 and, unlike many short-lived slogans, had a lasting impact on public opinion throughout the following decade. The ecologists even became a political force at election time. The alternative economic morality advocated mainly since 1968 is gaining wider acceptance and almost becoming part of conventional wisdom. It can be construed as a response to changed demographic and economic conditions.

SOCIO-ECONOMIC CHANGES

Sectoral redistribution took the form of a rapid exodus from the land, particularly in the 1960s. In twenty-five years the proportion of the active population employed in agriculture declined by more than half.* In 1956 over a quarter of this population still

---

*Another consequence of the rural exodus was the decrease of the percentage of women in the active population from 36 per cent in 1901 to 30.2 per cent in 1975 (*Le Monde*, 11 February 1977).

worked on the land; by 1972 only one in ten did, while four were employed in the secondary and five in the tertiary sector. The lasting importance of the rural population, which accounted for almost half of the French population at the end of the war, was undermined as the internal migrations that had been a continuous process throughout the century proceeded at an accelerated rate, accentuating the urban character of French society and aggravating regional imbalances. As the young have predictably proved more mobile, the demographic disadvantage of economically backward, under-industrialized areas has earned them the label of '*désert français*'. The choice between diverting resources from centres of growth in order to promote balanced development and concentrating them to preserve the country's ability to compete within the Common Market was difficult even before recession had begun. The fact that such a decision must be made by a centralized state bureaucracy throws some light on the limitations of regionalization as an administrative policy, regardless of the intensity of regionalism as an indication of the desire for a measure of self-determination – even for autonomy. Administrative decentralization is clearly inadequate as a response to such aspirations, which are directed not only against the Napoleonic state, but against the Jacobin concept of France, 'one and indivisible'.

In addition to accentuating regional disparities, the decline of agricultural employment necessarily entailed a transformation of the occupational structure. From the end of the war till the early 1960s it benefited both the secondary and the tertiary sectors. From then on tertiary employment – which by 1972 accounted for half of the active population – expanded at an unprecedented rate. Because of these occupational shifts, self-employment, mainly associated with small-scale farming and with the corner shops common in rural areas, has receded dramatically over the last twenty-five years. Consequently, wage-earners, who represented 63.7 per cent of the active population in 1955, constituted 84 per cent in 1977 (*Le Monde*, 27–28 November 1977) and the continuation of this trend is confidently forecast. The vulnerability of such a *salariat* to unemployment became evident as recession affected France and other Western European countries in the wake of the energy crisis. The expression of widespread anxiety and discontent has been mainly through party politics. The collapse of the *Union de la Gauche*, a consequence of the rift between Communist and Socialist parties, has entailed a weakening of protest against deflationary policies. Yet it is predominantly through political channels that working-class aspirations are formulated and furthered. This kind of politicization is linked with the relatively small proportion of union membership within the labour force (no more than 20–25 per cent), with its tendency to fluctuate and with the impact of the revolutionary tradition on French syndicalism. The fragmentation of the labour movement and the tension apparent in industrial relations have contributed to confrontation within the firm or the branch of industry rather than to the institutionalization of debate. It is significant that experiments in self-management, such as the Lip factory work-in, were derived from protest against both management and trade union practices. Another feature of the crisis in 1968 comes to mind: the dissociation between the *autonomistes* who disrupted factories and the Communist-dominated CGT, which brought its members back to work and contributed to the restoration of order in industry, particularly at the Renault works near Paris – an episode which set a pattern at the time and was to acquire symbolic importance. Meanwhile the increase in tertiary employment, even within the secondary sector, has added little to the strength of the French labour movement.

Like the implications of demographic change for the educational system, those of sectoral reallocation and occupational repatterning for class consciousness and action cannot be grasped without reference to persistent cleavages that limit the scope and affect the course of planned social change.

THE PERSISTENCE OF INEQUALITIES

The overwhelming predominance of wage-earning as a source of income should not be assumed to represent a trend towards the levelling of wealth. Indeed, wages represent the only asset of those manual or white-collar workers who do not own any real estate and are thus in no way cushioned against the effects of inflation. They have been at a considerable and constant disadvantage in relation to other social groups, including some skilled workers, who are owner-occupiers and whose properties have been increasing in value at a rate of 7–8 per cent per year. The acquisition of property through savings and/or inheritance has been the main anti-inflationary strategy in recent years and has clearly been unavailable to the recipients of lower incomes. As the scale of remunerations is relatively wide, with a rate of pay for *cadres* (managers) that is higher than that of their British or German counterparts, the opportunities for savings and investments during expansion have been considerable. Consequently, it is hardly surprising that inequalities of wealth in Franch should have doubled over twenty-five years (*Le Monde*, 18 April 1978). While less than 10 per cent of households account for 52 per cent of the country's assets, 50 per cent possess a mere 5 per cent. An OECD report described France as the most inegalitarian of its member countries with regard to income distribution, with the most affluent 10 per cent of households enjoying incomes 21.7 times higher than the poorest 10 per cent. However, these data were derived from income tax returns and enquiries into living standards. If the former source is discarded, the latter would yield a ratio comparable with that of other advanced industrial countries (Aron, 1976, pp. 500–1).

The divide between manual and non-manual workers certainly represents one of the main cleavages in French society. Yet its existence does not suffice to buttress the hypothesis that polarization is taking place or to challenge the credibility of reformist policies. The working class has actually decreased within the working population (from 66.7 per cent of wage-earners to 44.5 per cent) in the post-war period and the trend towards its reduction within the labour force has been steady since 1970. Some Marxist analysts challenge the criteria used by INSEE to demarcate occupational categories. By relying on the traditional definition of the worker as a wage-earning producer of surplus value, they widen this category somewhat and maintain that it still represents 55 per cent of the active population (Quin, 1976). Alternatively, the view is put forward that within the petty bourgeoisie small producers in agriculture, handicrafts and trade are very similar to the proletariat in terms of 'objective' interests and living conditions. While such an interpretation is compatible with Marxism, theorists of the Communist Party have put greater stress on the close relationship between manual workers and other wage-earners, white-collar workers, technicians, engineers, lower-grade managers, teachers and lower civil servants. These members of the somewhat elusive category of the wage-earning population sometimes described as 'intermediary' (*couches intermédiaires salariées*) are perceived as 'children of the new forces of production', the closest allies of the classical proletariat. This thesis differs from the views of such sociologists as Alain Touraine, who holds that it is from among these strata, and the students destined to join them, that the new revolutionary class (taking over from a declining proletariat, numerically depleted and attracted to the consumer society) is to be recruited (Touraine, 1971). Yet the increase in semi-skilled employment might challenge this hypothesis, and the degree of deprivation experienced by the unskilled workers, often recruited from among foreign migrants, certainly does.

Undoubtedly, the concentration of immigrants in manual jobs (with approximately one million such workers and another million unemployed) is a reflection of the native workers' distaste for these strenuous and relatively unremunerative occupations. In turn, this trend towards the employment of foreigners has contributed to the lowering of the prestige rating of manual labour.* A special campaign to restore the status of manual work in society was deemed to be necessary, and the appointment of a Secretary of State responsible for the task was intended to co-ordinate official policies – which have not,

---

*The concentration of women in unskilled jobs is another relevant factor: between 1968 and 1975 their number increased by 27.7 per cent, while that of their male counterparts dropped by 10.7 per cent (*Le Monde*, 27 January 1978).

however, proved conspicuously successful. This failure is inseparable from the problems raised by immigration, which has increased throughout the post-war period, but changed radically in the 1970s, with a predominance of North African and Portuguese arrivals instead of the former inflow of Italians and Spaniards. More pronounced cultural differences, added to a more exotic outward appearance, contribute to the stigmatization of these immigrants, especially as they tend to congregate in areas where employment is more readily available. Over a third of the foreign population lived in the Paris area, according to the 1968 census, which assessed it at 5.3 per cent of the total population (while the foreign working population was 6.25 per cent of the labour force, with nearly two-thirds employed in the secondary sector). The presence, in already overcrowded urban and suburban zones, of this generally underpaid and un-integrated group, whose living conditions (especially with regard to housing) are much worse than those of the lowest French socio-economic categories, represents a considerable threat to unitary class action. Prejudice – particularly strong against North Africans, partly as a result of the Algerian war – may be described as a form of false consciousness, but is not exorcised by this formula.

MULTI-LAYERED STRATIFICATION

Despite the distortion entailed by the existence of immigrants at *lumpenproletariat* level, class analysis emphasizes the divide between a manual working class, supplemented over time by sections of disintegrating middle strata, and a bourgeoisie supported by the remainder of these strata. It does so at the risk of oversimplifying the compartmentalization of French society. Eluding classification to the extent that they include both wage-earners and self-employed producers, the *class moyennes* are notoriously fluid. Though self-classification may not be a particularly reliable source, it is indicative of the 'decomposition' diagnosed by Marxist sociologists. Out of three artisans and small shopkeepers, two consider themselves to be members of the middle strata and one of the working class. White-collar workers are equally divided between the two. Somewhat more surprisingly, one middle manager out of four considers himself working class, whereas less than one industrialist, higher manager or professional in four is prepared to be defined as bourgeois rather than as a member of the *classes moyennes* (*Le Monde*, 8 February 1977). Polarization is thus hampered by the proliferation of intermediary groups, among whom the main criterion of differentiation appears to be security of employment – demarcating the privileged at each level of the economic hierarchy. A generalized quest for individual safety leads to the premium placed throughout society on civil service posts. Even minor post office or railway officials enjoy a prestige incommensurate with their income level, but deriving from their state-guaranteed security. Higher civil servants – the product of the *grandes écoles* in which bureaucratic, political and economic elites are trained – occupy the top rung of the hierarchy of prestige, outclassing businessmen, despite their greater affluence. Academics have lost status since 1968, and teachers have experienced decreasing esteem since the fifties, when the difficulties of adapting the educational system to socio-demographic pressures became obvious. Somewhat paradoxically, qualifications dispensed by this system remain highly rated, provided they are scarce. It is at least partly by educational rather than purely economic criteria that the upper stratum or *classe dirigeante* (top managers, higher civil servants and a few professionals) is demarcated from the middle strata. Hence it is a small category, which tends to be self-perpetuating but which – through educational channels (*filières*) – co-opts 'good pupils' from among the lower bourgeoisie (Vincent, 1978), as was the case under the Third Republic. The meritocratic character of this elite derives from educational qualifications, but is fully compatible with a strong emphasis on social persistence. Recent research has shown that the 'new' managerial class is predominantly recruited from among former owners of large concerns or their sons. Intermarriage and concentration in the Paris area are among its traditional characteristics, as is the inflow of higher civil servants resigning to take up top positions in the private sector, especially in banking.

Such integration among the ruling section of the bourgeoisie perpetuates a tradition dating back to the Napoleonic pattern of elitism. It appears to contrast with the avowed commitment of both top officials and top managers to policies of social change. This underlying contradiction helps to account for the distrust with which reforms are frequently received, merely on the grounds of their origin. Such suspicions are clearly widespread in industry, where new approaches to management tend to be construed as the outcome of capitalist paternalism and technocratic authoritarianism and are hence resented by unionized labour. Innovation is resisted as a mere window-dressing for exploitive relations. 'Group paranoia' – to use Vincent's terminology – is conducive to the entrenchment of socially isolated groups, concerned with the protection of acquired rights and the pursuit of fragmentary goals. The compartmentalization of society can clearly be related to widespread ambivalence about the process of modernization in which all socio-occupational categories find themselves enmeshed, despite some attempted resistance to the authoritarian pattern of its inception and many sectional protests about its perceived consequences.

AMBIVALENCE ABOUT MODERNIZATION

In a number of respects optimism about the advantages available to individuals in an expanding economy outweigh the condemnation of growth as detrimental to vulnerable social groups, such as the small peasants or the workers in an unmodernized industry, as well as the owners of the least viable firms. It is only because public opinion accepted the rewards of planned change, despite the moralistic strictures of 1968 against its excesses, that after the events of that year the same policy could be implemented with slight modifications of style but without alteration of content. Under the Fifth Republic opportunities for upward mobility are felt to be increasing (by 57 per cent of the population and, most significantly, by nearly half of the working class) and lifestyles are considered to have improved sharply within the lifetime of respondents (four-fifths of the population, according to a recent survey under the auspices of the *Société Française de Recherches et d'Etudes Statistiques* – see Duhamel, 1978). The coexistence of these apparently contradictory views of social change, vitiated at source yet beneficial in its effects, helps account for the contradictory attitudes displayed towards social inequalities. Despite the persistence of egalitarian aspirations evidenced by the electoral behaviour of nearly half the population in 1978, and its attachment to the political parties of the left, traditional attitudes to property ownership (see *Institut Français d'Opinion Publique* survey – Arbois and Schidlow, 1978) and to the acquisition of educational qualifications can be traced back to the ideal of social stability and gradualism characteristic of pre-war France.

Individualism – the desire to derive personal gain from expansion and to protect one's children's future through the acquisition of property and/or educational qualifications as a key to social promotion – is a link between the preservation of traditional attitudes and the acceptance of modernization. It is compatible with majority support for innovatory policies in the economic sphere rather than evidence of an innovatory mentality within the population, since its target remains security for the small family group. Such an approach has often been stigmatized as 'petty bourgeois' and its generalization can be connected with the growth in size of the so-called 'new middle classes'. Depicted by Crozier (1964a) as 'la classe sans conscience', these strata – defined by reference to occupation and including middle managers alongside technologists and planners – have gleaned considerable rewards from the process of growth to which their activities contribute. Privatization and vulnerability to manipulation by the media have been blamed for the acceptance by this group of consumerism in an industrial society. Yet an alternative reading of their position is offered by Touraine (1966), who highlights the vulnerability of technologists to employer authoritarianism and their heightened awareness, within the firm, of the connection between capitalism and technocracy. The hypothesis of politicization in a period of economic recession, and hence of a *rapprochement* with the skilled working class, is tenable, although the pattern of trade union intervention in 1968 shows that such an alliance would serve to achieve tactical goals rather than structural change.

Ambivalence about modernization is, of course, reinforced by the ideological divisions within the labour movement. The cohesiveness of working-class values and attitudes, already undermined by objective differences in working conditions (between public and private sectors, between modernized and obsolete firms, between prosperous and crisis-stricken regions), in levels of skill and in ethnic background, is not enhanced by competition between trade unions. The union officials' preoccupation with retaining power over members acts as a brake on innovation in power relationships within the firm, as was clearly shown by the attitude of the CGT in 1968. The possibility of a rift between 'control-claim' unionism and 'wage-claim' unionism (Dupeux, 1976, p. 255) emphasizes the divergence between the political interests pursued by the leaderships and between the perceived interests of the rank and file. The heterogeneity of the working class, initially stressed by Mallet (1963) is both a product of France's economic retardation and a source of divergent attitudes towards growth. Mallet's 'new working class', employed in the more technologically advanced and less paternalistically run enterprises, was expected to display the greatest level of revolutionary consciousness. Confirming this diagnosis, Touraine (1966) stressed its high level of skill, its acceptance of automation and other new techniques and its militancy in pursuit of a less dependent role in industry. By contrast, the resistance exhibited by craft unions towards technological change threatening job security, and the concern of assembly line workers with wage increases, were both dismissed as reactionary, backward-looking attitudes. Yet the expectations of sociologists were actually frustrated by the course of the 'May events', since it is in the older types of industry and among the less unionized categories of workers that strike action assumes the greatest importance. Clearly, the 'new working class' has no monopoly of militancy and does not provide a pattern with which other sections of the same class seek to identify. The concept of a compartmentalized society is yet again more acceptable than that of polarization, whether between or within classes. Hence the difficulty of singling out, through class analysis, the section of society from which modernizing innovation emanates as distinct from all those which accept it with varying degrees of reticence.

THE SOURCE OF INNOVATION

The coexistence of conservatism in values and attitudes with the innovatory policies and practices which enabled France in three decades to make up for a prolonged period of low productivity and delayed industrialization is a puzzling and much discussed aspect of post-war social change. The impact of the baby boom on the size of the active population was only experienced in the late sixties. Until that date the active population remained constant, so that growth did not affect outputs. The shift into secondary and tertiary occupations has been accomplished in the context of governmental policies, often imposed upon reluctant participants by state action and always involving a change in the relationships between the state and the main economic actors. Undoubtedly, entry into the EEC helped France to overcome the handicaps of economic retardation by subjecting industry to the stimulus of international competition and by providing agriculture with a more favourable price structure, as well as with an extensive market.

However, it is through state-initiated reforms within France that the resistance of historical constraints to demographic and

economic pressures has been circumvented, lessened or overcome. The planning process provided a new framework for the
operation of industry, encouraging some concentration of firms
and providing various forms of assistance to establishments
situated in priority regions or engaging in selected areas of
operation. Furthermore, the spirit of *concertation* on which
indicative planning rested has provided a training ground for the
participatory practices later developed in response to, and as a
containment strategy for, the power-sharing demands of 1968.
Yet state intervention has persisted, at the request of both
employers and unions, despite the lip-service paid to greater
decentralization in the decision-making process. The tradition of
recours à l'Etat (reliance on the omnipresent state) dies hard,
whether in industry or in agriculture.

In the agricultural sector the impact of state policies on the
increase in average farm size, the growth of productivity and the
adoption of modern techniques has been considerable. It has
been furthered by the coincidence between these goals and the
stance adopted by the CNJA, harnessing the more militant elements of the 'new peasantry' to the pursuit of modernization. An
analogy could be drawn with the influence on policy formulation
of the CJD, reflected in the Sudreau Commission's report. The
emphasis on promoting dialogue and involving the groups formerly deprived of any say in the workplace can be related to the
legislation on the collective bargaining process. However, it is
undoubtedly in this sphere that the access to decision-making
opportunities has appeared most strictly limited by conservative
attitudes – exemplified, despite the rhetoric of the CNPF, by a
majority of employers, but exhibited also, for the reasons
already indicated, by trade union leaders.

The focus on state initiatives is not tantamount to an endorsement of the view that all innovatory practices have been
introduced 'from above'. The contrast posited by Crozier
'between the negative and conservative behaviour of all formal
groupings, and the effervescence and intellectual, irresponsible
creativity of individuals' (1964b, p. 286), appears overstated. A
number of the groups involved in the modernization of the

business firm and of agriculture production have displayed both the willingness and the ability to innovate. Yet it must be granted that they represent the exception rather than the rule, that group attitudes towards modernization have been characterized by an ambivalence bordering on timorousness and that departure from traditional practices can usually be achieved only with the support of state intervention. It is probably true that such support is generally secured by the political astuteness of creative individuals. Thus, in his discussion of planning structures, Crozier (1965) stresses the original contribution of Jean Monnet and the small team which surrounded him, '[who realized] intuitively that they could only succeed if they put themselves at the service of the business world and of the Administration and sought, in exchange, to secure their help instead of trying to force them into compliance'. To accept this 'great man' interpretation does not in fact challenge the crucial role played by the power-holders, whom 'creative individuals' have to convert, manipulate or in some way convince that their innovatory insights further the course of planned modernization. The effervescence of ideas has been, no doubt, the prerogative of individuals – both talented and well connected. In this respect the family background of Monnet in French business and his international political connections can hardly have been irrelevant to the scope of his influence. Thus a stress on individual creativeness is fully compatible with a recognition of the links between elite groups. Ultimately, however, the responsibility for the dissemination and the implementation of innovatory ideas has rested with the state throughout the post-war period.

STATE-DOMINATION AND PLANNED CHANGE

The domination of society by the state, accompanied by the distrust of 'intermediary groups' between state and individuals, which is an inherent part of the French revolutionary legacy, has frequently been diagnosed as a major factor behind the retardation of the economy prior to the Second World War. Its intervention has furthered the development of the main economic sectors and has promoted modernizing practices, at the risk of imposing them upon unwilling participants. Thus in the immediate post-war period it was the content rather than the form of state action which appeared to have changed. Yet the contradictions inherent in pursuing the ends of modernization through the means of the centralizing, hierarchical administration of the Napoleonic era could not easily be reconciled. Under the Third Republic it was possible to rely on the operation of the administrative and the educational machinery for economic protectionism and social entrenchment. In the words of President Deschanel, 'We have the Republic on top and the Empire underneath.' It was doubtful whether such a time-honoured formula for stability could prove compatible with the pressures of population growth and the strains of occupational redistribution, accompanied by geographical mobility.

That this incompatibility was perceived to some extent under the Fourth Republic is evidenced by the reform aimed at democratizing recruitment into the higher civil service through the creation of the ENA, as well as by a series of attempts to introduce a measure of vocationalism within the school system. Yet the Napoleonic tradition of elitist selection proved enduring and somehow capable of accommodating some of the requirements of the expanding economy. The endurance of the traditional *grands corps* in the administrative sector is clearly in contradiction to the post-war emphasis on unifying the civil service. Yet it provides a means for supplying the specialists needed in an age of quantitatively expanding and qualitatively diversified state intervention. The transition from generalist to specialist administrator, which has not yet been satisfactorily effected in Great Britain (see Sheriff, 1976), did not constitute an issue in France, since specialized training could coincide with, and indeed result in, traditional prestige through membership of an elite corps. The *grandes écoles* illustrate a similar pattern of retaining elitism while updating vocationalism. Thus the Empire endures 'underneath', and meritocratic arguments serve to legitimate traditionalism.

The other aspects of the Napoleonic legacy – authoritarianism and centralization – have been historically linked with the values and attitudes of the administrative elites. In fact, they could be considered inseparable from the structuring of the French state under the monarchy, since Tocqueville has shown that they were furthered for centuries by the Bourbon dynasty and merely incorporated into the Jacobin ideology. Hence it is hardly surprising that the connection between nation and state – predating, as it does in France, the age of nation-states – should have become inextricable. Faced with the double challenge represented by demands for the recognition of ethnic, cultural and economic diversity within the French Hexagon and pressures for the involvement of citizens in decision-making processes, the Fifth Republic has responded with policies of regionalization and participation. Administrative and educational reforms have been adopted in response to societal unrest, climaxing in the events of 1968. Thus, in a sense, they correspond to the definition of change 'through crisis' posited by Crozier. Whether, in fact, they amount to more than piecemeal rearrangements, compatible with the persistence, under a refurbished façade, of Napoleonic structures, is a highly contentious issue. It has been the main source of debate about the pace and the scope of change in France throughout the seventies.

Even while it is recognized that it is state action which has provided the main source of change – either in pursuit of developmental objectives or in response to protest – the question remains open of whether reforms have merely served to defuse tensions and protect the continuity of 'Napoleonic' power structures. One approach to participation is to detect in it a mere strategy for containment through the securing of more information for the traditional decision-makers, while socializing those consulted into accepting the fiction that they are actually involved in the formulation of policies. The Machiavellian view is that this is a mere device for tension management, coupled with a means of gauging the receptiveness of the public to bureaucratic activities. State policies can thus be made more acceptable, both because they are perceived as less remote and because they are more likely actually to incorporate inputs from the people, particularly at the regional and local levels.

An alternative view stresses the innovatory characteristics of any deconcentrating and participatory measures (by contrast with the Napoleonic model). It focuses on the formative impact they may have on those administered, as well as on the administrators themselves. The reconciliation of the contradictory trends towards conservation and towards innovation is sought in gradualism. It is hoped that – to paraphrase Rousseau's tenet about citizens being 'forced to be free' – groups will, through consultation, learn to be innovatory. To accept such an interpretation requires confidence in the genuine commitment of rulers to planned change extending beyond limited economic objectives. Hence optimism about participation and the related target of regionalization virtually amounts to an endorsement of Mannheim's belief that political issues could ultimately be turned into 'problems of administration'. Inherent in theories of bureaucratization, this 'neutralization' of power is as ideological as its systematic distrust, enshrined in Machiavellian theory. Ultimately a choice between the two hypotheses is conditioned by philosophical predilections; it is a value-judgement on which all evaluations of facts depend. Even if one accepts the contention that reform is limited by the administrators' judgement of its acceptability rather than by vested interests alone, it is difficult to deny that enlightened despotism endures in a novel form. 'True reforms are those which, unconsciously, are already in the mind of the French. They are then credited to a man, a party or a regime' (Guichard, 1975, p. 165). Whether the state as psychoanalyst is less authoritarian than in its Napoleonic garb would suggest may be a matter for speculation. That it is no less paternalistic seems obvious.

BIBLIOGRAPHY

ARBOIS, J. and SCHIDLOW, J. (1978) *La vraie vie des français* (Paris: Seuil).

ARON, R. (1976) *Plaidoyer pour l'Europe décadente* (Paris: Laffont).

BIRNBAUM, P., *et al.* (1978) *La classe dirigeante française* (Paris: PUF).

CROZIER, M. (1964a) 'The cultural revolution', *Daedalus*, 93 (1), 514–42.

CROZIER, M. (1964b) *The Bureaucratic Phenomenon* (London: Tavistock).

CROZIER, M. (1965) 'Pour une analyse sociologique de la planification française', *Revue française de Sociologie*, VI (2), 147–63.

DOGAN, M. (ed.) (1975) *The Mandarins of Western Europe. The Political Role of Top Civil Servants* (New York, London: Wiley).

DUHAMEL, A. (1978) 'Le consensus social', in J. Jaffre *et al.*, *L'opinion française en 1977* (Paris: FNSP).

DUPEUX, G. (1976) *French Society 1789–1970* (London: Methuen).

DYER, C. (1978) *Population and Society in Twentieth-Century France* (London: Hodder & Stoughton).

GUICHARD, O. (1975) *Un chemin tranquille* (Paris: Flammarion).

MALLET, S. (1963) *La nouvelle classe ouvrière* (Paris: Seuil).

QUIN, C. (1976) *Classes sociales et union du peuple de France* (Paris: Editions Sociales).

SHERIFF, P. (1976) *Career Patterns in the Higher Civil Service* (London: HMSO).

TOURAINE, A. (1966) *La conscience ouvrière* (Paris: Seuil).

TOURAINE, A. (1971) *The May Movement* (New York: Random House).

VINCENT, G. (1978) *Les jeux français. Essai sur la société moderne* (Paris: Fayard).

WYLIE, L. (1963) 'Social Change at the Grass Roots', in S. Hoffman *et al.*, *In Search of France* (New York: Harper & Row).

Abbreviations

ANDA	Association Nationale pour le Développement Agricole
CE	Comité d'Enterprise
CEG	Collège d'Enseignement Général
CELIB	Comité d'Etudes et de Liaison des Intérêts Bretons
CES	Collège d'Enseignement Secondaire
CET	Collège d'Enseignement Technique
CETA	Centre d'Etudes Techniques Agricoles
CFDT	Confédération Française Démocratique du Travail
CFT	Confédération Française du Travail
CFTC	Confédération Française des Travailleurs Chrétiens
CGA	Confédération Générale de l'Agriculture
CGC	Confédération Générale des Cadres
CGPME	Confédération Générale des Petites et Moyennes Entreprises
CGSI	Confédération Générale des Syndicats Indépendants
CGT	Confédération Générale du Travail
CGTU	Confédération Générale du Travail Unitaire
CIAT	Comité Interministérial pour l'Aménagement du Territoire
CID	Comité d'Information et de Défense
CJD	Centre des Jeunes Dirigeants
CJP	Centre des Jeunes Patrons
CNAT	Commission Nationale de l'Aménagement du Territoire
CNJA	Centre National des Jeunes Agriculteurs
CNPF	Conseil National du Patronat Français
CODER	Commission de Développement Economique Régional
DATAR	Délégation à l'Aménagement du Territoire et à l'Action Régionale
DEUG	Diplôme d'Etudes Universitaires Générales
DP	Délégué du Personnel
ENA	Ecole Nationale d'Administration
FAFEA	Fonds d'Assurance Formation pour les Exploitations Agricoles
FDES	Fonds de Développement Economique et Social
FEN	Fédération de l'Education Nationale
FIAT	Fond d'Intervention pour l'Aménagement du Territoire
FNSEA	Fédération Nationale des Syndicats d'Exploitants Agricoles
FO	Force Ouvrière
FORMA	Fonds d'Orientation et de Regularisation des Marchés Agricoles

GAEC	Groupements Agricoles d'Exploitation en Commun
GIF	Groupe Inter-ministériel foncier
IDI	Institut de Développement Industriel
INSEE	Institut National d'Etudes Statistiques et Economiques
IUT	Institut Universitaire de Technologie
IVD	Indemnité Viagère du Départ
JAC	Jeunesse Agricole Chrétienne
JOC	Jeunesse Ouvrière Chrétienne
MODEF	Mouvement d'Organisation et de Défense des Exploitations Familiales
MRG	Mouvement des Radicaux de Gauche
MRP	Mouvement Républicain Populaire
ONIC	Office National Interprofessionel des Céréales
OREAM	Organisation d'Etudes d'Aménagement d'Aire Métropolitaine
PADOG	Plan d'Aménagement et d'Organisation Générale de la Région Parisienne
PCF	Parti Communiste Français
PMI	Syndicat Patronale des Petites et Moyennes Industries
PS	Parti Socialiste
SAFER	Société d'Aménagement Foncier et d'Etablissement Rural
SDR	Société de Développement Régional
SFIO	Section Française de l'Internationale Ouvrière
SICA	Société d'Intérêt Collectif Agricole
SOPEXA	Société pour l'Expansion des Ventes des Produits Agricoles et Alimentaires
SSE	Section Syndicale d'Entreprise
UDCA	Union de Défense des Commerçants et des Artisans
UER	Unité d'Enseignement et de Recherche
UNATI	Union Nationale des Travailleurs Indépendants
ZPIU	Zone de Peuplement Industriel ou Urbain

Author Index

General Index